T0171706

DEADHEAD

THE BINDWEED WAY TO GROW FLOWERS

JERIANN SABIN
RALPH THURSTON

authorHOUSE®

AuthorHouse™
1663 Liberty Drive
Bloomington, IN 47403
www.authorhouse.com
Phone: 1 (800) 839-8640

Published by AuthorHouse   02/12/2016

ISBN: 978-1-5049-7967-2 (sc)
ISBN: 978-1-5049-7968-9 (e)

Other Books By Ralph Thurston

No Sage: Essays From the Margin

Leaving the Bucket: Searching For the Sacred in Addiction

Loving Allis Chalmers: Essays From Agraria

Open Range: Grief, Humor, Music and Other Occasions

CONTENTS

Part 1: The Bindweed Way 1

    Introduction 3

    The Importance of Ignorance 6

    The Importance of Uncertainty.............13

    Assessing Your Resources 17

    Points of Sale 26

    The Things You Need......................... 33

    Delivering Flowers 37

    Getting Answers................................. 45

    Vices You Didn't Know You Had..................... 49

    Method—Vice, Virtue, or Both? 56

    Slack.. 60

    Windows... 64

    Scale 67

    Testing the Waters 71

    Employees (I Saw You Shudder) 74

Part Two: The Bindweed Handbook...................... 77

    Introduction 79

    Harvesting and Processing.....................81

Season Expansion 89

Seeding and Planting.. 95

Growing in Crates...103

Weeding...106

Perennials 113

Annuals 138

Bulbs 155

Uglies and Foliage 165

Woodies 172

The Tools...180

Part 1

THE BINDWEED WAY

INTRODUCTION

Deadhead—in gardening, the act of cutting spent blooms from flowers to either keep them from going to seed or to inspire re-bloom.

Deadhead—a trucking term referring to a return trip with an empty load.

Deadheading can be a bad thing, it can be a good thing. From the perspective of a trucker, who only gets paid for delivering goods, deadheading means no pay but plenty of expenses for driving an empty truck. But to a flower farmer who sells his own flowers on a bucket route, deadheading means the day has been a success— he's sold all of his product and he can whoop and holler and celebrate on the way home.

To a flower farmer deadheading also means work (maybe a bad thing), but not more work than he'd have if he didn't do it (so, a good thing). Removing spent blooms means seeds won't form, fall and become plants in unwanted places in too great of numbers, and it also promotes more blooms.

Most everything in the natural world and on a flower farm operates just this way, good in one sense, bad in another, with one climate good for one species and bad for another, another climate just the reverse for the two. One soil wrong for some varieties, right for others. A method perfectly suited to one project ill-used when applied to another.

And then there's the business world and the fashion world that a flower farmer's operation abuts, where what's in one year is out another, what one person likes another hates, where favorite colors change and design styles radically differ.

Everything's a moving target.

Starting out flower growing, you have to step out into that whirling mass of change and determine just what's going on, where every obstacle is, where you are in relation to them. It's a dance, maybe even a dance where you have to juggle as you make your moves, and you have to find a way to move comfortably and deftly as you participate.

This book is about growing flowers in one place in one time in that dance. If each of the hundreds of American growers wrote a similar book about their place and time, you'd have a pretty good view of just what flower farming and marketing is all about. By itself, this book may only be marginally helpful, but if you apply its contents to other information you glean and knowledge you already have it should assist you— especially if the conditions where you farm approach those on ours.

Several years ago an employee made shirts for our farm that read "Bindweed Farm—Established 1990-ish" on the front and "The Bindweed Way: 9104 experiments, 0 mistakes" on the back, referring to our philosophy of shrugging off goof-ups and turning them into ways to acquire new knowledge. We move fast on Bindweed Farm, so often plant in the wrong place, plant the wrong seed, mix up seeds, and in general, make a lot of mostly small mistakes. But each time we do the results tell us something: that "wrong" way of netting turns out to be "right", better than our usual method. That species we mistakenly planted early actually thrives in cooler weather than we thought. We've learned a lot from our mistakes, and we hope this book inspires you to make some mistakes of your own, as well as learn from ours, so you can be deadheading your way home with an empty truck and a sense of satisfaction.

THE IMPORTANCE OF IGNORANCE

If I took you back in time to show you how Jeriann and I became flower farmers, you wouldn't believe we would ever be making a living, much less a good living. Our knowledge reservoir didn't register empty but came close—I'd grown up on a dairy farm and worked on a two thousand acre potato and grain operation for a decade, but I couldn't tell my peonies from my asters.

Our first farm, loaned to us by Jeriann's parents, was an old riverbed that sported fist-sized gravel so plentiful it provided enough drainage for a neighbor's pump to run all summer without creating a pond. Our infrastructure included a five horsepower tiller, a hoe, a shovel and a rake. We sold from the hatchback of our car and then—Woohoo!—from the back of a pickup with a camper shell. We had no cooler, just utilized the basement in the high heat of summer to keep flowers cool.

With high hopes, I sent out letters to over thirty prospective florists in the valley announcing our operation, and received not a single response. Failing there, we persevered, selling at a farmer's market twenty miles away, sometimes only making thirty dollars a day. The first summer I sold fresh flowers on a bucket route I made about four hundred dollars selling to mom and pop shops and florists in our hometown—less by tenfold what we may make at a single stop now.

Our ignorance was a blessing, because had I known how pathetic our operation really was I would have quit.

The story I tell tracing our steps from near nothing to two hundred thousand dollars in annual sales might well be fiction since neither I nor Jeriann can recall exactly how it happened—not because we have Alzheimer's, but because events happen so quickly, erratically and organically on a farm that they defy memory.

Since a teenager, I raised leafcutter bees, a valuable insect that pollinates alfalfa seed, but over time commercial agriculture became more efficient, farming from road to road, eliminating fencelines, tree lines and all wild areas, shrinking forage area for bees. In an attempt to keep the bees thriving, I planted two acres of wildflowers on my in-laws' unused property to create extra habitat. Since Jeriann was artistic and interested in dried flowers, I added a small plot of about eight hundred square feet for that project, planting a hundred small packets of different species from a dried flower seed specialist in hopes of finding out if leafcutters preferred one flower over others, with a secondary hope that the flowers might be harvested and sold (though to whom, I had no idea—I hadn't gotten that far).

The field was stunning (if you ignored the weeds) and from the tiny plot of never-before-seen-by-us flowers, some wholly unsuited to our climate and soil, Jeriann made wreaths that we sold at craft fairs that winter, enough to justify further trials. We shortened the list of drieds, eliminating obvious failures, increased their area, and expanded our sales from craft fairs to a local farmer's market and a couple craft stores.

It seemed an easy step from growing drieds and selling them at the farmer's market to picking a few fresh flowers to have along with our offerings, since we were already growing some varieties usable as both, like larkspur and statice.

And when a florist showed up at the market and bought a few things and asked us to stop by her shop, it seemed a no-brainer to expand our fresh flower sales to a bucket route that included other area shops.

And when we saw other wholesalers at the florists it seemed it might be easier to sell exponentially more product to them, even if at half the price.

And then when one of our wholesale buyers sold out and another went broke, we had to think fast or get real jobs, so to stay in business we realized we needed to copy and tweak what they had done. We'd learned enough in conversations and a short stint working for a wholesaler during the Valentine's Day rush to see that the resort designers bought far more flowers, particularly the kinds of flowers we grew, than the area florists we were selling to, and so we decided to do a bucket route that catered to the resorts.

And we haven't looked back.

After two decades of mistakes we now make a good living working from mid-March to mid-September. We owe nothing on our house, our land, our vehicles. We grow ninety-plus species of flowers, shrubs, bulbs and grasses on about four acres, all in a zone five climate with only 120 days between the last frost in May and first one in September. Almost half of our sales come in two months, July and August, with earlier sales supplemented by a couple of heated greenhouses, each two thousand square feet, a hoophouse of equal size, and a three thousand square foot shadehouse. Selling to about twenty clients in two mountain resorts within two hours driving distance, we make fifty trips a season.

Jeriann and I do almost all of the work ourselves, me on the beast end of things in the field, she on the beauty end attending to processing and clients, sales and service, though we have two part-time employees who work 600 hours a season washing buckets, driving an extra van on the route, weeding and spraying and helping with all the odd jobs associated with a farm. If you don't include our hours in the expense column, we cleared a hundred thousand dollars last year, a big difference from that first summer of four hundred dollar sales.

And did I mention we get November, December, and January off, and only work a few hours in February,

March and October? And part-time in April and September?

If you're thinking about flower farming, you're probably leaving a job, tired of working for someone else and longing to be your own boss. But if you're like me, you might discover that working for someone else probably wasn't as bad as you thought and you may be embarrassed at how bad an employee you were. You may come to sympathize with your former employers once you act from a position similar to theirs. When you work for yourself, you can call in sick and you can leave jobs undone and you can even do them poorly, but you and no one else will pay. When you're the boss no one rides you about your performance, or inspires you, or lays out your day, and there's no one else to point fingers at, no one to whom to complain. And if you hire help, you may find that being an employer is just as emotionally wearing as being the employee.

On the other hand, there's nothing like taking a break when you feel like doing so, grabbing a bite when you're hungry, and not having to answer for every movement—you may find that the freedom of working for yourself outweighs the increased responsibility, though there'll be days when you wish you could turn the farm off and it would all just go away.

Once you make the choice to turn from employee to entrepreneur, you'll need to start building an empire, with networks of associations with customers and service people, plant and plug vendors. You'll need to develop an infrastructure of devices you may not be familiar with: tractors, tillage equipment, coolers. You may have to hone your people skills and better your work habits. As you grow and learn you'll inevitably run into the difficult decisions that come with opportunity, as hoe turns to hand tiller turns to tractor, as back yard turns to leased land turns to purchased land, as air conditioner turns to cooler turns to bigger cooler and yet a bigger one, as row cover becomes greenhouse, as delivery van becomes truck, and along the way you may find that everything you do was in some way a mistake: if you'd only known, you'd have bought more land, built more greenhouses, built a bigger shop, a bigger cooler, not planted that woody. Unless you want to be buried by regret, you'll laugh all that off.

How do you get from there to here? Well, it's like the old question, "how do you eat an elephant?" The answer: "one bite at a time." We couldn't have envisioned what we've become, couldn't have imagined we could actually do the amount of work we do or sell the amount of flowers we sell. But here we are, and we'd like you to get here, too, because the world's a better place when people are running their own show, reaping the rewards (and yes, disappointments) of their labor, feeling responsibility and freedom simultaneously, and most importantly, being out in the natural world and feeling the sheer joy as each new species comes to bloom. There's really nothing like it.

So we'll start with a few chapters of broad generalizations that might help you gather your wits and ready you to tackle that elephant you so want to eat. Then we'll get to more specific techniques that work for us, as well as telling you about those things that haven't panned out so well.

THE IMPORTANCE OF UNCERTAINTY

You know how drug commercials promote a product for fifteen seconds and then detail the side effects for the next forty-five? Well, we're going to start off just the opposite, with the disclaimer first and the sales pitch at the end. Because that's the way it's going to work if you choose to start farming: the punishment comes first, then the reward.

If you're thinking about going into flower farming, well, you're probably going to fail. Most new businesses do. If you think you're a great manager and can just hire help to do the unpleasant work, well, you're probably wrong—you're not as good a manager as you thought, and the help you need most likely only exists in your mind. If you've watched "Field of Dreams" and think "if you build it they will come", well, maybe you should stick to watching movies.

I'm trying to discourage you because I hate seeing people attempt things way out of reach and fail. I want you to be realistic, and that means acknowledging your shortcomings, acknowledging the enormity of the task ahead of you, and acknowledging your ignorance. The good news is that your ignorance works in your favor, allowing you to go forward into the great unknown of flower farming.

Once, waiting to give my own presentation to potential flower growers, I listened to the speaker before me emphasize the need for a business plan when starting out, and my first comment upon beginning my own speech was "forget what he just said". Not that planning is evil in itself, but just like chaos, if taken to an extreme it has bad outcomes. Every time I sit on a Board and hear someone harp about the need to create a committee or the need to create a "mission statement", I cringe, because the way to get things done is to DO THEM! It's easy to get lost in the planning—just remember yourself as a child, when you spent hours preparing play scenarios that lasted a fraction of the time it took to plan them (if they happened at all).

Banks, the Small Business Administration and financial advisors want to see a plan, though, those itemized steps on paper they're so comfortable with because that's what they do all day—they operate in a world that's static, one where risk is predictable, and they have formulas assessing it allowing them to plug in numbers you give them and regurgitate a yes, we'll lend you money, or no, we won't. That's how they shrink their risks and limit their failures—and blame what failures they do have to the formulas given them.

If you've already met with lenders and been frustrated, congratulations—you're on the right track. Your intuition tells you something's askew, giving you a bit of wisdom they lack: you're operating in two different worlds, they in risk and you in uncertainty.

Frank Knight detailed the difference between the two nearly a hundred years ago, recognizing uncertainty to be the only place real opportunity for profit exists. Risk is knowable, coming from a set of mathematical outcomes from the past (think the throws of a dice— over time, you can be sure you'll throw an equal number of ones, twos, and so forth), and only mature industries or businesses, where the cost of nuts and bolts is fixed, wages are static, expenses are given and have been for some time, can assess risks and fiddle with numbers until they make a plan profitable—but if you watch the big dinosaur businesses, you'll notice all they're good at is cutting costs or buying other companies smaller and more deft than they are.

But you're operating with uncertainty, with no givens from the past, and that uncertainty means you can't know or assess probable outcomes. You're guessing. Just guessing. You just hope it's a good guess. The good news: you already knew that, but thought there was something you were missing.

You may be frustrated to discover there's no easy answer. But you shouldn't be, because you've been feeling this uncertainty for some time, I'll bet, as excitement on one hand and fear on the other, and you've been waffling back and forth from day to day, one moment eager to take the leap into farming, the next afraid of what farming might entail. But now that you know that your feelings are perfectly rational and not just you being crazy, you can step past that queasy mixture of anticipation and angst toward action.

If you really could plan a successful flower farm just by putting down the steps on paper, don't you think everyone would already be doing it? To be sure, you should make a rough plan but make a plan B and plan C, and leave a big section in each for the off the cuff actions you'll have to take, the switches you'll have to make, the alternatives you'll have to find, your improvisations. Farming, even more than regular businesses, requires dexterity, being subject not just to nature's changes but the fickle trends of fashion.

So if you're ignorant and uncertain, you have two essential qualities of joining the flower farming kingdom.

ASSESSING YOUR RESOURCES

Demographics

Before you start you can help yourself by finding the demographics of the area you're going to serve. If you plan to sell to individuals or those who cater to individual customers remember than women who make over fifty thousand dollars are the primary flower buyers. If you live in Pingree, Idaho, where I grew up, population 150 (none of the residents millionaires, so far as I know), that means you're not going to have a lot of customers to sell to, but if you live within two hours of two separate resorts where the number of millionaires per capita exceeds most anywhere in the United States, you have a shot at marketing cut flowers and making a business successful. That's where we are, but we didn't know it until after we'd already started, we just got lucky. Good old ignorance.

You'll want to go to either the local university or any government entity that's business oriented to find the necessary statistics. They're still not likely to come to you on a silver platter, so you need to get used to the painful process of working through the minor difficulties of ferreting out information. When you don't get an answer you need at one place, look in another, keep pestering the people you've already pestered, change the frame of your question—the information is there, you just have to find it. (Funny enough, ours was in Time Magazine's International Edition, which I was perusing when we lived in Ireland in 1992, just before we began dabbling in flowers—a map displayed nearby resorts as the only two blotches in the intermountain area with very high concentrations of wealth. Unfortunately, it didn't occur to me until over a decade later, when we were already selling in the two places, how useful that information was. Ignorance again.)

Finances

To start any endeavor you need resources. If you have plenty of money you probably aren't reading this, but certainly money is a great resource when it comes to starting a business, and having money, land, or equipment helps a great deal on a farm. But even if you lack these, you likely possess skills and traits you might not call resources but which in fact help a great deal in operating a business.

How To Knowledge

Horticultural experience or knowledge helps. What do you know how to do? Transplant, irrigate, fertilize? Have you grown a garden? Do you use and arrange cut flowers? Are you familiar enough with plants to know the difference between species and cultivars, do you recognize fertility problems, the presence of pests? You may know more than you think you know, and if you are willing to learn what you don't, believe it or not that's an asset.

Aesthetics

Do you have any aesthetic sensibility? Can you tell fuchsia from cerise, lavender from violet, salmon from coral, *and* can you describe that difference to clients or employees? Even with the advanced technology that allows you to send pictures instantly to clients, it's still helpful to be able to verbalize color. For example, the spectrum of hues called purple extends further than you might believe (we grow a Zinnia that some clients call purple, some call pink, and others call lavender) and that's just one slice of color. Business exchanges will suffer if you provide the wrong color even if you are right and the customer wrong when judged by the Pantone scale.

Do you know which colors work with others? Which complement? Which contrast? If so, your clients may eventually depend on you enough to give you a color scheme for which they trust you to provide different flowers. Do you know what current trends are and what they'll be? You may become the person your clients rely on to provide what's new and exciting. All those years you thought you were wasting time thumbing through fashion magazines may come in handy, after all.

Sales and Service

Are you a people person? "Schmoozing" requires a natural talent that makes a client feel comfortable with you, and each client has different needs, different levels of tolerance, different topics of interest. Some may be no-nonsense while others need to know how your kids are. The better you are at assessing others and the more abilities you have in interpersonal interactions, the better you'll do at sales. If you're not good at these things you'll do better if you hire someone who is (unless you're married to someone, that is, as I am).

Land

Do you have land or access to land? Is it good land? Does it have enough water? We started out on Jeriann's parents' land, leased to us for free, which was a good thing because we had nothing, but we quickly learned that the omnipresent gravel made it impossible to weed. We then rented a small acreage with good soil, but the weeding hours became insurmountable due to the constant supply of new weed seed coming down the irrigation ditch. And dealing with the landlord was so painful that we timed activities around his absence. Only when we found our own acreage and used drip irrigation did we realize how easy farming could be, and we cultivate our entire acreage in less than fifteen hours a week, half that we spent on a plot a third the size.

Experience in the Field

Do you have experience in the floral business world? Have you worked on a farm? For a designer? In a floral shop? For a wholesaler? Do you know someone who does? A yes to any of these helps a great deal, otherwise you either need to learn on your own the ins and outs of the segments of business you'll be aiming at, or work closely with someone already involved. Get some experience, work for a short time in the business, get a price list from a friend who works for a designer, go to conferences, get a part-time job, go to farmer's markets, spread your network to include anyone who might provide information. Be patient.

You really need to know how much risk you are comfortable with, so form a spectrum in your mind that runs from no risk to full out anything goes, and put yourself honestly where you belong. And then be comfortable with your choice.

Stuff

You'll need infrastructure. Delivery vehicles, tillage equipment, A COOLER, and a gazillion smaller items too numerous to mention. With a proper business plan and unlimited resources, of course, you'd know exactly what to get but since you have no idea how successful you'll be or what problems you'll run into you need to decide which way you'll go: overcapitalize or undercapitalize, meaning spend a lot for the perfect thing or start out small and cut your losses if you fail. Maybe your ideal dream is to have a semi truck full of flowers going out every week, or maybe you're content to drive a bucket around in your Volkswagen Beetle passenger seat. You might succeed with either method, but more likely you need something in between. Assess your *needs* in a way that separates them from your *wants*: sure, a mechanical transplanter would be nice, save a great deal of work, but does the size of your operation justify the cost? Do you really need a machine to do a job you can do by hand in a few hours, or do you just think it would be really cool to have one?

We always choose conservatively when making a large purchase, buying something adequate but which can be upgraded in size if business grows. We've moved from a minivan to A Dodge Sprinter to both and then to a Sprinter and a larger Ford Transit, with a mini Transit for smaller, local deliveries. We moved up from a tiny, two-door cooler to an 8' x 20' cooler in much the same manner. Financially, the long-term *perfect* decision would have been to have the bigger units from the start, but since we were afraid of spending money and losing it if we failed we chose to take smaller losses as we traded vehicles and coolers. The right short-term answer may not be the right long term answer, but it may very well be the proper answer at that time.

Tractor

Eventually, to get your farm from hobby to livelihood, you'll probably need a tractor. It's a big expenditure, difficult to make if your budget is small, so you might try to get by with a big hand tiller when you start, but having a tractor increases your time efficiency and makes easy work of tilling that a small tiller finds impossible. Maybe you'll find a used tractor that doesn't cost ten or twenty thousand dollars, but it might not be the bargain you think unless you can fix it when it breaks. Since I inspired the no-mechanic-left-behind bill pending in Congress, I chose to buy a new tractor, a 29 horsepower, four wheel drive New Holland with gears slow enough to comfortably walk aside. The slow gears are essential for the work on a flower farm, where tight quarters are the rule, and four wheel drive helps when tilling deeply with a ripper or chisel plow or in soft soil conditions, or when using the loader for moving mulches and manure or dragging or pushing snow in the winter.

Assessing your Assessment

While assessing your personal resources is important, more importantly assess your assessment: be honest with yourself. Maybe you're a fantastic mechanic, but do you work on others' projects before you do your own? Or maybe you're a whiz with numbers and think you can do your own taxes, accounting and payroll—but will you actually sit down and do all that work every month, or will you get lost in the farm work, something you find more enjoyable and will usually seem more pressing? If you want to succeed you have to admit your virtues AND your vices—you can only overcome the latter by acknowledging and working around them (I'm going to assume you can't change them).

Old Vs. New

A local farmer, one of the ten largest in the nation, decades ago decided to buy new equipment and replace it regularly, rather than hang onto old equipment that, while paid off, inevitably would require repair. He has scores of semi trucks, grain combines and spud harvesters, but owns a repair shop little bigger than those on farms a tenth the size. Sure, new equipment costs more than old, but only until you factor in the cost of repairing broken machinery, the parts and skilled workers needed to fix it, the time lost holding up harvest or planting, the product lost. By trading in his used equipment, he exports the difficulty of used equipment to others who either can't afford new or believe themselves to be in a situation where they can beat the odds by doing their own repair.

So, if you're not going to fix your own infrastructure, don't buy old equipment that may need repair, buy new equipment, because even though you CAN fix problems you WON'T. If you aren't going to do your payroll and accounting in a timely fashion, let someone else. Don't undertake projects or make purchases that may require skills you have but likely won't use.

So you'll need a lot of things, a lot of skills, but maybe you have more resources than you knew you had. And, you know the ones you don't have.

POINTS OF SALE

Farmers markets are a good place to start, and a good market can be a mainstay even for established growers. We began fresh flower sales at a market selling a few skimpy bouquets from our car, coming away with thirty dollars, a great deal of compost and skepticism about the venture. At the opening bell our sale sign read one price, was soon crossed out and replaced with a lower price, then crossed out again. Had other vehicles not boxed us in, I'm sure we would have left not just the market but flower farming forever.

But we persevered, made bigger bouquets, established a clientele by continuing our presence, keeping quality, and discovering what people wanted by paying attention to both successes and failures. We were eating that elephant one small bite at a time, and eventually, after a couple years, we were selling three to five hundred dollars a market on high peak weeks. We added a market in another, more affluent city, the same distance from us as the first, giving Jeriann the new gig knowing that she, being more personable, would likely do better. Funny thing was, I usually doubled her sales.

Another grower attributed this to "the cougar effect", claiming that her sales increased whenever a young man staffed her booth. She said that since older women were the typical customers, they just naturally bought more from a non-threatening man than they would from another woman.

One thing to remember about farmer's markets is that, just as no one takes the last piece of pizza, no one grabs the last bouquet. Customers shy away from scarcity—when you see a store with half empty shelves, aren't you a bit skeptical of the place and the product?—so you need to have more flowers than you plan to sell. When you're down to the next-to-last bouquet, give the last one away with it—you'll create a customer for life. Flowers are always a luxury, so your booth needs to reflect that: explode with color, exhibit lushness, keep your booth clean.

You may have a natural inclination toward not throwing things away and think that it's better to sell most of what you take rather than sell more and waste more, but any successful restaurant owner will tell you that you never want to run out of a product, that customers buy from plenty, that waste is simply a logical cost to figure in when you establish the price of your offerings. And, if you want to think about it in a more scholarly way, complexity theorists have shown how this snowball effect exists in almost all systems, including economic ones, mathematically showing that more begets more, that the more cars are parked in a parking lot the more cars will come into it—it's a flocking phenomenon that you may personally not follow (I for one shy away from lines and crowds, but I'm obviously an anomaly) but which most of your customers innately move toward: your clientele forms just as does a sand dune, one grain inspiring another to stop and then another and then another, so make your display lush and plentiful and expect to take some product home.

After you appear at farmer's markets for a few weeks or years, you'll inevitably encounter designers and florists who will hear about you from their customers. Couples wishing to do their own weddings and people wanting to do events will approach you, as might photographers and painters needing something to spruce up their subject matter. Your network has started and you might find it more appealing to make the rounds selling flowers to clients who buy more at one stop than to sell one bouquet at a time to forty or fifty different customers. You may tire of dealing with a constant flow of people, even if you LIKE to deal with people, you may weary of standing on hot pavement, fighting high winds, enduring late snows, you may tire, too, of making bouquets and seeing them go to waste at the end of the day and opt for a bucket route, in which you take consumer bunches (a set number of stems of a single species of flower) in water to designers on a set day. As a wholesaler with a bucket route you'll have fewer customers but larger orders.

Subscription bouquets can be a profitable foot-in-the-door for a grower. Even nearby Blackfoot, with a population of ten thousand, has a hospital, courthouse, dentists, doctors, lawyers, banks, government offices— all of them needing flowers. You may want to maintain a weekly vase of flowers free of charge, with your card identifying you as the designer, at a place with lots of foot traffic, generating advertising far more valuable than the flowers themselves. Community Supported Agiculture provides a similar outlet, with your customers paying you upfront for a season of bouquet deliveries.

Selling to wholesale buyers is another option for flower growers. As a grower I've long dreamed of just harvesting all my flowers and selling them all to a single buyer who'll give me a decent price that keeps me involved in my addiction. But I have to admit that my desire has no relationship to reality.

The reality: a wholesaler–grower relationship entails precariousness for the grower, as any agreement generally places all risk on him. After a wholesaler told us he'd want five hundred sunflowers a week we planted accordingly, but at harvest time he ordered a third of that. A grower can't change his mind after planting but a wholesaler can. He has scores of other, larger growers at his door and when Ecuador offers ten cent roses he'll choose those over yours, and when thirty cent delphiniums come available from a bumper crop in California he'll choose those, so unless you share some personal loyalty with him, lean toward healthy skepticism—don't bet the farm on a handshake, and be prepared with another market should you lose your wholesalers.

But a good relationship with a wholesaler can be lucrative, and we sold to several over the years with varying degrees of success. Because so many people get into flower growing and perhaps try to get into markets before they're ready, wholesalers may look at you skeptically and be resistant to buying from a new grower. Be persistent. We faxed our availability to a large wholesaler every week for years without success, and one day, as I was hoeing weeds in the field, that wholesaler called me wanting to look at the farm, as his usual driver had taken a vacation and he had taken over the route.

When he came out and saw our farm and witnessed its well-kempt state, he immediately began buying from us. Coming from Montana with a load of flowers for delivery to Southeast Idaho, he returned to Montana with a load of ours—this saved him the expense of trucking comparable flowers from California, giving us a more attractive sales position. Funny enough, the same flowers we sold to him on Thursday that rode to Montana came back through Southeast Idaho and were sold to local designers on Monday.

The reward of selling large amounts to just two or three wholesalers can be outweighed by the power they hold over your business—if one goes broke, you lose that sale and without a place to move your flowers to you may go bankrupt, too. Having a larger customer base rather than a few wholesalers means having more but generally smaller headaches and risks. If one or two small clients go broke, you can more easily absorb those losses.

When a wholesaler we sold to went broke (a Valentine's Day left her holding sixty thousand dollars of the clientele's unpaid bills) we found ourselves in the position of losing two thirds of our business. Luckily, the failure came in the spring when we could easily make the transition from *selling* to a wholesaler to *being* a wholesaler, taking over some of the same routes and selling to the same customers with the same flowers but at double the price.

It was the best decision we ever made; I wish I could say we made it intentionally.

In our first year of sales on the bucket route, we sold three times what we had the previous year. We grew fifty percent the next year, and a third more the next. It turns out you can sell your own flowers better than anyone else can if you have good product and a good salesperson (thanks, honey). But we would never have known had we not tried.

Craft store sales taught us a great deal about chain store marketing structure, and though we still don't know much about the ins and outs of working with large companies we know enough to not want to do it. It took a great deal of effort to get a manager of a dried flower department just to look at our product, then more time for the manager to consult her boss who had to get with the warehouse manager. And even when we were successful in establishing a relationship of continual sales, if the first level manager quit we needed to repeat the process with the new hire—who likely found it easier to deal with a larger distributor than us. Our experience with the dried chain led us to refrain from ever trying fresh sales through corporations, though one of our biggest customers now is an independent grocery store, an entity with a shorter purchase chain and more deft than a big conglomerate.

Because supermarkets have so many customers you have a much greater client base, even if it's second hand. If you can get a good relationship with the flower kiosk manager, you can sell a lot more flowers than you might at a small designer's shop, where walk-ins may number less than one tenth of one percent of the numbers walking in a small supermarket.

At some point in time, unless you only sell to one segment of the flower industry, you'll run into conflicts between clients from different tiers. A wholesaler may be upset that you sell to his customers; a designer may be peeved that you cater to customers she perceives as hers; shop owners won't want you to sell to supermarkets, thinking them unfair competitors. You'll want to think about where you stand before this conflict occurs, because it is inevitable—locally, the largest potato distributors in the world face the same problem of miffed customers at different sales levels trying to force their hand. There's no ameliorating both sides, if one side presses the issue you have to make a choice. Don't think you'll avoid the problem, but have an idea of how you'll deal with it ahead of time.

THE THINGS YOU NEED

No flower farm exists successfully without a cooler. You can get by, but each advance in the quality of your cooling system affords a couple extra days of marketing time for your flowers. You trigger a time bomb every time you cut a flower stem and you can't keep it from going off, you can only delay it by proper conditioning and cooling. A cooler lengthens the marketing time of harvested flowers from a day or two to two or three weeks for some species, and mutes the noise of that ticking clock that is in the mind of anyone who deals in perishable commodities.

When we began we thought we could get by without a cooler, before realizing how cheap it was to rent a two door soda pop cooler from a beverage distributor. Then we thought we'd struck it rich when a client sold us a larger, used floral cooler for a hundred bucks, but that gold mine turned out to be fool's gold when we needed to replace the compressor a week later. Right then I vowed to never be lured by either used equipment or cheap buys.

Think about it—one instance of a cooler malfunctioning and freezing its contents can result in a loss equivalent to the cost of a brand new cooler. Not only do you lose those flowers, you weaken your bond with your clients—they'll trust you just a little less when you don't provide them with their needs that week. Even though we choke at the cost of a cooler every time we upgrade, we remember to put it into that mathematical perspective. And you will need to upgrade, I assure you, because a cooler is like a closet or a garage, or, you'll find, a greenhouse, no matter how big you make them they're never big enough.

Coolers can quickly lose their value, much like new cars, and may even become almost worthless or impossible to resell. Knowing this before our first big splurge, we bought a ready-to-go self-enclosed unit deliverable by semi, which we plugged into the garage's 110 volt outlet within seconds of its arrival. If you've seen 4' x 8' units on trailers running around your town, probably filled with ice servicing convenience stores, you'll know the type. Because they're so omnipresent we knew they'd be resalable if the business failed (our cooler, of course, had a compressor and cooling system for cooling flowers, not for keeping ice at below zero). The easy delivery and instant installation was a godsend for us, and by building a shelf inside the cooler we could hold three or four thousand dollars worth of product— slightly under the cost of the unit. We initially bought that first unit intending to mount it on a trailer to drive to the farmer's market, but lucked into a bucket route before doing so. We very soon needed a second one and had it in a week after ordering. When we upgraded to a larger, permanent cooler, we sold the self-enclosed units in very short time for a price much better than a used component cooler would bring, since the ease of moving them works perfectly for someone in a pickle needing an immediate fix.

We didn't know it (well, Jeriann knew it) in the early years but a small transport vehicle to run around the farm is pretty handy, if not essential. Rather than walking from field to processing area with each load of flowers, get a used golf cart for one or two thousand dollars and build a small platform or box on the back in which to put buckets, flowers, tools and the like to make your job easier and faster. For over a decade I walked everywhere on the farm, each armload of flowers a three or four hundred foot walk one way and the same amount back, each trip to check the driplines an unpleasant trudge as the day progressed, every maintenance event a frustrated and angry walk back and forth when I forgot a tool I needed. I don't know how I did it without the cart, but having it has eased the workload considerably. If you are a real fixit guy, you can even extend the chassis on a golf cart and turn a small bed into one equivalent in size to a pickup.

You can also rig up a cart to perform spraying duties, though we've not done so. Situate your walk rows so the cart easily maneuvers between flowers and save a bit of walking.

You probably think you need a pickup truck, but we get by without one. I wouldn't have believed it, either. The delivery vans provide the same service as a pickup—I only miss one when hauling stinky garbage to the county dump or getting gas and diesel cans for use on the farm. And for real dirty lifting we have a loader on the tractor.

DELIVERING FLOWERS

It's a long day for Jeriann when she drives the bucket route—two plus hours driving there, three hours selling flowers, moving buckets, negotiating tourist traffic, and the return trip on top of that, but when she compares the day's take to what we earned in prior endeavors she rarely complains. Sometimes pre-orders fill her van, so an employee drives a second one. Occasionally, if a big event is on the docket, a third delivery is necessary. At four, five, even six thousand dollars a trip, the stress of driving, schmoozing and getting things exactly right shrinks, particularly compared to what an hourly wage might bring for an equivalent time.

The first day we drove the treacherous Teton mountain pass, it had six inches of snow and slush (in June) and as I nearly slid off the summit I told Jeriann she didn't need to undertake the route if she chose not to (I would have quit, luckily she didn't). Not knowing what to charge for our flowers, we guessed, and the buck and a quarter a stem for peonies—half the going price—probably turned the customers' eyes when normally they would have dismissed us. The seclusion of the resorts that makes them appealing to the jet set creates difficulties in shipping that we took advantage of—at ninety dollars a box to fly flowers in, our high quality product became even more attractive. And Jeriann's exuberant personality and aesthetic sense, developed over her lifetime in art, decorating, cooking and every aspect of her being, prepared her for the pace-setting styles of designers in the high-end resorts.

Not everyone will be so lucky as we are, but we do have a few tips that might help out.

The optimum way to deliver flowers is fresh cut in water, since a moment out of water for a flower is similar to one for you with your head *under* water. They breathe water just as you breathe air, and they're dying! Nonetheless, they can hold their breath if properly hydrated, so can be shipped in boxes, out of water, and survive even a day or two later (depending on the flower type). A bucket route delivers flowers in buckets of water, whereas most shippers box up flowers and send them through the pipeline—sometimes a long flight, a rest at an airport, and a long trucking spate that could entail two or three weeks from cut to consumer use.

Keeping flowers cool, between 35 and 45 degrees, prolongs their life, so a refrigerated van serves best to transport them, but Jeriann was lucky enough to meet a D.C. grower who served his clients without refrigeration. Knowing our climate wasn't as hot as D.C.'s, we opted for air conditioning. Since our deliveries finish by one or two o'clock, the flowers have only been out of the cooler for five or six hours, but to maintain quality we compost return flowers (friends and family often are recipients of returns)— an advantage the grower-wholesaler has over typical wholesalers.

Some bucket routes actually use buckets, the five gallon type sold at Home Depot or Lowe's or scavenged from bakeries and grocers, but nearly twenty percent of the space of an area stays unused with round buckets. We use a few square buckets—also scavengeable from restaurants and bakeries—but primarily utilize Proconas, a rectangular container invented specifically for flowers that fit side by side and end to end without losing any space. The Procona system includes containers of different size increments that actually allow them to be stacked without loss of space, and has cardboard collars of varying heights that fit into the lip of the bucket. A lid fits over the top of the collar to make a nice seal, and also provides a platform on which to stack more Proconas. The collar protects flowers from breaking as they do when left unprotected—it doesn't take much of a jolt when buckets are shoved around and transported to knock a head off or bend a stem. We rarely stack the Proconas (sometimes in the cooler when short on space) but we frequently put smaller buckets of sweet peas and such on top. Between 25 and 30 Proconas fit our delivery van box (roughly four by eight, plus the area ahead and behind the wheel wells), and you can throw a couple on the seat and a few small containers between the seats.

Large flowers like Sunflowers present a problem even for Proconas, so we purchase wastebaskets (rectangular, not round) sizeable enough to hold fifty stems. Long stemmed Clematis, Amaranth, grasses, and other tall product go in these, too.

Small flowers like Sweet Peas present another specific delivery need, so we collect yogurt and cottage cheese containers to hold these, and hardware stores carry small, plastic buckets for paint that are perfect for short flowers. It helps vase life to keep flower heads above the rim of any container, the added openness an aid to air movement that helps them stay dry and reduces bruising.

While we're discussing buckets, let me admonish you: don't be stingy! Spread your containers around, mark them with your logo and your telephone number— can you think of better advertising? We tag ours by spray painting the rims red and advise our clients to pick a color and tag theirs, too. We buy extras and sell them to clients at cost, making bucket trading easier. Even if you gave away buckets with your deliveries, the five dollar (or less) bucket is just a ten percent markdown of the flowers you've just sold them. Most clients are glad to return your buckets, just make it a habit to retrieve them at each stop. When delivering pre-orders, it's much easier to drop off flowers, buckets and all, exchanging them for buckets left the prior week rather than taking ten or twenty minutes to move flowers from your buckets to the client's. If you waste those minutes at every stop, you've added two hours to your route.

Many growers leave a walkway on the van for clients to peruse the flowers, but because we travel so far we feel that's a waste of space, and though it's a reach to the far wall that may tax your acrobatic abilities (Jeriann does "truck yoga"), the seven or eight hundred dollars of extra product overwhelms that displeasure.

Sometimes clients forget something, or get a call from someone an hour after Jeriann's left town, or sell out of snaps or suns the same day as delivery and can't wait a week for more. That's when it's time to send flowers in a box.

UPS, FedEx, DHL—everyone knows these shippers, and for long distance flower sales you'll be using these companies, but local couriers often carry goods cheaper and faster than the big three for nearby sales. We rarely ship to clients outside our area, primarily because we're not interested in expanding to that level and hiring another employee to provide that service, but our standby customers often need flowers on off day deliveries. Their clients may call from the East Coast on a Sunday to have their vacation home filled with flowers on Monday when they fly in, and there's no way to get flowers from California or elsewhere if they've not been ordered the Friday before, so we become the go-to source by default. Our local courier picks up boxes of flowers the first thing in the morning for afternoon delivery in one resort, and picks them up in the afternoon for overnight to the other, and best of all, picks them up at various times of the day for more local deliveries with just two or three hours between pickup and delivery time. The use of shipping expands our sales by twenty percent.

If you worry about shipping because you're a novice, pack a box of flowers and send it to a friend or family member you trust, then ask them for appraisal of what's arrived. This information eliminates the uncertainty you may have about quality standards.

To ship, you'll need boxes ice-packs and newspapers. We bought a small number of flower boxes from a large provider of California shipping material when we started, and found that the cost of shipping the flat, cardboard boxes was as great as the boxes themselves. We then took the plunge of buying an entire pallet from a supplier much closer, realizing that despite the cost over time we'd be better off. We also recycle boxes that our clients set aside for us, sometimes coming home with a truck full of empty boxes if there's room. Big companies charge for boxes and packing, but we do not. After all, we're making two to four hundred dollars a box—what's a five dollar box and a few minutes of packing? Every extra charge adds to the confusion of a business interaction and reminds the customer that she's incurring debt—keep the relationship simple. We do pass on the shipping costs, however, for which our courier charges about twenty dollars a box.

We also get recycled ice packs from our clients and have never actually had to buy them! We ask friends and family to save newspapers for rolling up more fragile flowers like snapdragons or bulky ones like tulips which want to be compressed to keep them tight and less likely to break, and also so more will fit in a box. The newspapers wrap the ice packs, too, to protect flowers from freezing on contact.

Twenty good clients provide us with a good living, with our largest client usually making up 20 to 30 percent of total sales. There's a wider client pool out there, but we require a minimum purchase to weed out smaller customers who may require as much maintenance as bigger buyers. It can take as much time and effort to make a thirty dollar sale as a two thousand dollar one, so if your time is finite, you may have to turn smaller customer away. We discourage on-farm pick up because customers often want to see the business—and we want to show them!—but that time bomb is ticking in our head, telling us all the other things we need to be doing. We've also discovered that a lot of do-it-yourself brides are really do-it-yourself-cheap brides, so we're leery on first contact, and even when big purchases take place from international designers flying into one of the resorts, we find that the exchanges don't go as smoothly as those with trusted clients. Our attitude may seem ruthless, but an operation that's set up to move product quickly and smoothly can really start to sputter when it confronts a slow exchange with little profit.

Cheaper is not better. It's difficult for a grower to see uncut flowers in the field, worse to see them dying in the cooler, all the work of planting, growing, and harvesting withering away along with profit, but dropping the price ultimately works against the grower for a number of reasons, particularly since demand for a perishable product cannot rise significantly enough to overcome lower prices. If you sell twice as many flowers at half the price, all you've done is doubled your work and decreased your profit margin. Stand your ground on price or you'll join the race to the bottom, and WalMart has already won that. That said, part of what got our foot in the door was low prices.

But we didn't keep them low.

GETTING ANSWERS

If you don't know something, ask someone who does. And if they don't know or are reluctant to share, keep asking. No one likes to appear ignorant, but if you ARE ignorant there's only one way around it—ask questions! You may feel ridiculed or belittled but if you don't ask or try you can only stay the same. If you are made to feel small and worthless, you're not asking the wrong question, just asking the wrong person.

Even bad information can be good. If someone suggests you grow poinsettias for the Christmas season, or Easter Lilies for Easter, you probably can place them in the questionable source column, since you most likely can't compete with megastores who sell those items at a loss. If you have an idea, ask the bad sources and if they think it's good, toss it. We've had a source tell us sunflowers were out of fashion (fifteen years ago—we're still selling suns), that only tall flowers sell (we may actually sell more short flowers, dollarwise), and that oranges and reds don't sell during the summer (we sell tons of orange Asclepias), so we tend not to trust her advice.

The place to learn about flowers is the Association of Specialty Cut Flower Growers. You'll recover your membership dues in confidence and sales. Maybe you're used to joining organizations that cost (and provide) very little so the fee seems high, but this organization is like no other, its members span much of the globe and someone out there, somewhere, has already run into any problem you might encounter and will likely give you advice. It's like having not one mentor but hundreds. Without the ASCFG, we'd never have gotten off the ground, for no amount of Internet searches (which weren't even around when we started) will give you information as quickly or accurately as this organization. Remember, if you get just one bit of knowledge, one single tip, your investment return will justify a lifetime membership. Don't think of saving money, think of making it.

Buy Judy Laushmann and Alan Armitage's book, Specialty Cut Flowers—also known as the "Bible" for flower growers—the best source for growing cuts. You may not find everything there, but you'll find information that would take you weeks or years to find on your own. Lane Greer and John Dole's book, Woody Cut Stems for Growers and Florists, is handy, too, if you're working on woodies. And subscribe to Growing For Market, a newsletter that'll bring huge return on your investment by identifying new trends and old methods (new to you, however) in both flower and vegetable farming.

When we began, we knew next to nothing about flowers, so the ASCFG, through its membership, is really responsible for most of our success. We piggybacked on the knowledge of other growers, utilizing their techniques and applying them to our own situation, putting us decades ahead of where we'd be otherwise. Membership in the ASCFG opens up many doors with just a click of the mouse.

Ask other growers questions. If this fails or if you're too timid, watch them. Follow their posts on the Internet. A great deal of academic research is detailed regarding specific species and though much of this research takes place in California, North Carolina or Georgia, you can take information from your situation and adjust the data found there to your operation.

Weather constrictions were a major thing to consider when we looked at such information, as Georgia and California don't really have the same temperatures as cold Idaho. But they do have frost dates, average highs and lows, and by finding theirs through Internet searches we could simply substitute their dates of planting and harvest with ours—for example, if our last frost date is May 15 and theirs is March 15, we just move their instructions forward sixty days or so and act accordingly. There are tweaks to make in the adjustments that include northerliness (which affects hours of sunlight), light-days (a measure of cloudiness in your area), humidity averages and such, but if you are familiar with even one species or two in your region, you can compare the differences between your knowledge and the information given about that species in other regions, then apply those differences to plants with similar habits and needs. You'll find a set of plants that match your soil, weather conditions, light availability, and discard from your list those species that will be certain mistakes (but if you're like us, you'll still try a few things you shouldn't).

As important as shadowing other growers' actions was for us, it may have been more crucial to our operation to get connected with others in the industry. Speaking with others about their farms and techniques spurred ideas of our own, and often what we heard opened up entire new avenues for us as our own situation presented possibilities through the new information we were given. Every bit of contact you have with the outside flower world provides you with information, and even negative information is useful in that you know what and who to avoid.

VICES YOU DIDN'T KNOW YOU HAD

One of the most important things I ever heard was "every virtue can also be a vice". You know the virtues of ignorance and uncertainty, now we'll look at the vices. You probably operate with a set of virtues that works well for a household budget, like saving money, but while that works well when you live on a fixed budget, being in business means your intention is to make money, not save it. A householder thinks of his budget as a ceiling which he must stay beneath, but a businessman needs to work above that ceiling with the intention of continually raising it.

It's not how much you sell, it's not how much you buy, it's the difference between the two, so consider this—it may seem expensive to buy a three dollar plant when you can buy a much smaller one for a buck, but who cares what the cost is if you triple your money with the three dollar plant just three months later, while you have to care for the dollar plant for a year to achieve the same result? A three-foot tall viburnum shrub may seem expensive at ten dollars, until you start cutting two dollar stems from it a couple years later, and ten years later cut forty and fifty stems each season. When making expenditures, think of the money you'll make, not the money you save. Farmers who pinch pennies are farmers who soon go broke because their attention has strayed from their aim of making money. Caught up in the magic of the bargain, they've lost focus. That doesn't mean, of course, that you go all out and spend every penny you have on anything at all that turns your fancy. Just keep your eye on profits, with less of an obsession to costs. Treat any expenditure toward money-makers differently than you would toward expenditures that might be necessary but will never generate income.

Another problem that comes when moving from a household to a business budget is the sudden differences in dollar amounts. That thousand dollar invoice for plant material might spike your blood pressure because you're thinking of an equivalent bill when running your home, but you have to remember that the decimal point moves at least one slot since it takes money to make money—your household never actually makes money, your farm does. You may never get over the habit of trying to save a nickel here and there when you see what things cost (I caught myself working the lumber yard on the price of a dozen 2 x 4's, for crying out loud), but you need to train yourself to look at purchases with a different perspective. The difference in cost between a good piece of farm equipment and one of lesser quality may be recoverable in less than a year, and a cheap, used cooler can cost you the price of a new cooler when it freezes its stored product.

Buying new might be the right thing, but you don't need to grab every gadget or technological advantage. You don't need every tool—it might be nice to have a socket set, a ratchet-wrench set, a pair of vice grips, a set of end wrenches in both metric and American sizes, but will a couple adjustable wrenches suffice? Maybe you'd like a welder, but how often will you use it? Is there someone nearby who could do your welding work? Even if you have a tool, it might be cheaper and quicker to have someone do the work for you—we often hire a rotovator even though we have two of our own, as I may be busy doing other things and the cost of having it done isn't that much more than the cost of having me do it.

That brings us to another vice, selflessness (here you thought it was a virtue). Your work and time isn't free and shouldn't be treated as such. If you think it is, you shouldn't be in business because you can't see hidden costs. Put a price on your time, a high one, and realize that a twenty minute delivery run into town costs you an hour, costs mileage on the vehicle and wear and tear on your already frayed nerves. Even if you'd be napping, that nap's not worthless, you need your rest and the cost of losing that time means something—monetize it. A happy, well-rested you is a valuable commodity, an overworked you loses worth quickly in not just the ill-will you might spread to the operation but the mistakes that accumulate when you're overwhelmed.

Perfectionism, yet another vice in the wrong place, takes you down the road to insolvency. So can being sloppy, of course, but that vice already gets plenty of press. Let's just take a couple of examples, flower preservative and flower cutting.

Preservative companies have a chemical solution to every flower hydration need. There's a great deal of research on prolonging vase life with chemical preservatives that I don't dispute, but we buy one all-purpose powder and do just fine. You may not need a different concoction for every species if you move flowers from the field to the client quickly enough. Your flowers don't need to be perfect, just better than your competitors', so if they don't move product quickly and don't use proper storage protocol throughout the sales chain, your imperfectly conditioned flowers may still be better than theirs. The grower can't change the bad habits accruing down the flower chain, his perfectionism in preparing flowers can't overcome the sloppiness of those that follow him.

This may be a lesson of the A– grade, which Jeriann now repeats to me after I've repeated it to her over the years: as you move from A– to A+, you move from low cost to high, minimum effort to maximum. Unless you are paid for perfect product in accordance with its costs, you lose money as you improve. Find the sweet spot where high quality comes easily and don't work your tail off or expend resources to go beyond that place.

Another virtue that becomes a vice is the urge to conserve. The household virtue of saving things needs to be replaced with an equation that measures not just if something can be used, but if it WILL be used, if it will take up space, how much time and energy will be spent retrieving and maintaining it. Keeping a piece of wood, plastic netting, used drip tape, old plug trays—things that are saved may just clutter your farm and your mind. For instance, returning from a route with unsold flowers that must be composted, we recycle but do not reuse the sleeves taken off the bunches. Old sleeves stack poorly, if at all, and any flower diseases upon them, however unlikely, don't go away but spread. The time it would take to do the right thing, re-use them, results in costs to the business greater than that of new sleeves.

How much time does it take to recondition or prepare something you saved ten years ago because you knew you'd use it someday? What does its new counterpart cost? Weigh the two options not as free against costly new, but as the cost of your time and reconditioning against that new item that may last longer.

If you consider yourself "green", you'll be fighting the idea of waste pretty consistently, because making money often means wasting things. I can save tulip bulbs each year to use them again, but the monetary cost of caring for them—re-planting, irrigating, weeding—until they produce a marketable product exceeds the cost of new bulbs: do I remove the old bulbs and buy new ones or go "green" and shrink my profit margin by saving old ones? Is the carbon footprint left by using plastic drip tape larger or smaller than the alternative of using ten to twenty times as much water with a different irrigating system? Am I wasting precious resources hauling in sludge to amend my soil, or is my action greener than the more distant trucking that the sludge would have undergone had I not used it?

There is no fixed good and bad when it comes to environmental concerns, just better or worse. Any action results in disorder somewhere, negatively impacts the world somehow, and any substance in the wrong place or amount can be a pollutant. There is no perfect solution, just better ones. Till as little as possible, re-use when you can, shrink your impact, choose manual over mechanical labor, consider actual, rather than ideological, results of every action—work toward the ideal while staying real.

This is counterintuitive to an environmentalist's moral imperative, but much of capitalism is. You'll have to find where you're comfortable on the scale that runs from all-out capitalist to one-with-nature and be good with the results of your decisions. Choose what works for you and be happy, but as a flower grower it's hard to take the moral high ground. After all, that ground I farm could be better put to use growing vegetables. Every time we load a van and use ten gallons of gas for the flower delivery, I think of the waste of fuel—but we're closer than California, closer than Ecuador, closer than New Zealand—hopefully, the ten gallons we use is less than the amount to fly in flowers from the other side of the world.

Don't be cheap. Pay your help well—don't you expect fair pay? A good employee makes you money and a bad one costs you.

Pay an accountant—they don't cost you money, they make you money with their expert knowledge. One timely tax tip may save you all the money you'll pay your accountant over a lifetime.

Pay experts to do things you don't do well. If you aren't good at germinating seeds, you're not saving any money doing so, so buy plugs. Pay someone else to do something better and more cheaply than you can—can you really pay attention to seedlings for ten weeks or more, checking them every few hours for moisture, coping with fungal issues, paying for seeds, trays, and media for less money than the ten or twenty cents it costs to buy a plug? Only if you love germination and are good at it should you undertake that task.

Be generous. Every once in awhile give your clients some flowers "just for them", not for their shop. It may seem ridiculous to give flowers to a flower shop, but you'd be surprised how pleased even designers are to be given flowers. And if you have a variety someone's unfamiliar with, give her a bunch or two to play with the first week it's on so she gets a feel for it—in the long run, it's an investment for you that may pay off big if she likes it.

Treat generosity not like an item on the expense column but one on the income side, since giving is your gain and it's infectious to those around you.

METHOD—VICE, VIRTUE, OR BOTH?

I don't know if all businesses have this characteristic, but flower farming certainly does: a set of methods that exceeds the abilities of one human to possess them all. Working with plants requires one set of skills, but selling flowers requires another, and it's not that common to find both sets in the same person. Luckily, as a couple, we've got it covered: Jeriann has the latter and I the former.

If you do try to do both things, you may find one way of thinking gets in the way of the other. When we started and I both grew and sold, I'd be thinking about selling as I was out in the field, thinking about irrigation and weeding and cutting as I was out selling on the route, doing a disservice to both ends of the operation. It's hard to make a proper customer interaction when your mind's twenty miles away on your farm, and it doesn't help the farm much when you drop what you're doing to run into town to make a sale.

Luckily, Jeriann took over the sales end, freeing me from the split-brain existence I'd been suffering. Not only is she more personable and thus better with customers, she understands color and texture enough for clients to depend on her for inspiration, two invaluable skill sets that give us a leg up on competitors whose delivery people only know how to drive and drop off orders.

Jeriann and I happen to be like oil and water when it comes to our philosophies on method, so our business union may not have worked if we didn't realize the irony and absurdity of working together—or maybe it was just forbearance on her part that let us succeed. She's a perfectionist, raised by an engineer father who insisted things be done correctly, trained her to break tasks down and use proper tools and methods. On the other hand, I come from peasant stock that survived the Depression and World War II, who hardscrabbled the land and used baling wire, twine and wits to keep a farm and family together. While I get things done, she gets things done RIGHT. Fortunately, the two of us meld the two extremes, because without her perfectionism we wouldn't have our reputation for quality, and without my overbearing urgency to just get things done we'd never have had a business at all. A flower farm needs both kinds of thinking and doing to succeed.

In regards to planning, she jumps from idea to plan immediately, laying out a sequence of actions with a quickness I marvel at, while I avoid plans like a vampire shuns light—I bristle not just at following others' plans but upon encountering my own.

But even those of us who don't plan have structure, otherwise we'd wake up and fly to Prague for an espresso rather than go out to the field and cut the flowers, weed, irrigate, spray and market. Most things dealing with nature require a deft flexibility that defies planning, but method comes to prominence in the inorganic realms of finance and business. If your clients expect you on Monday morning, you need to show up on Monday morning, and if they expect twenty bunches of orange zinnias you had better show up with that many orange zinnias—not coral, not salmon, but orange. And if you say a bunch of zinnias costs eight dollars, ten bunches had better cost eighty because your billing needs to be exact. Every mistake you make mars a customer's impression of you. Your color understanding needs to be spot-on, not almost right.

When you run into disagreements regarding structure, and you will, remember that while the philosophical problem of how much planning and method is enough isn't resolvable, understand that your smaller problem IS. Give up being right. Be satisfied that a job gets done and finished on time even if it's done with a way that differs from yours. And don't get in the other person's business: if she's the salesperson, don't interfere with the clients, and if he's the mechanic, don't be moving his tools.

Speaking of method, if you're a gadget guy, you're probably a method guy. It's a good thing, generally, to have a way of doing things, since by splitting a task into parts and arranging them in order you may be able to do it better, and if you have to do the same task multiple times it's a way of saving you the effort of having to learn how best to do it again and again. Even those of us who say we lack method actually may have it, it's just that we assimilate ours into the unconscious so we don't have to think about it.

However, method becomes a vice when it gets in the way of action. If you need to hammer a rebar into the ground, why not use a nearby rock to pound it in rather than walk three hundred feet to the shop for a hammer. Save yourself time (though costing yourself the comfort of having the perfect tool), because if your way of doing things gets in the way of getting things done, it's not helpful.

Likewise, if you buy every tool that's perfect for every occasion, you'll end up with a barn full of tools. Do you really need that cool dibbler in the latest catalogue, or can you just use your finger—or a stick—to make the ten thousand holes you need each year for planting plugs? It's easy to overestimate how much technology you'll need if you're in love with the illusion of machines fixing every problem. Think low input, maximum output when you decide what to buy and use. You can run a farm with a lot less than you imagine—no one believes we run our farm with our meager shop: an incomplete end wrench set, some screwdrivers, pruners, scissors, hoes, shovels, all fitting on one wall with room to spare. Many people have more tools just for do-it-yourself projects.

SLACK

We're going to call it slack. Somewhere in academia someone's studied and given it a better, more accurate term, but we'll use "slack". It's something akin to "wiggle room".

What's slack? Well, let's take cutting flowers as an example. If you only plant a hundred tulips and tulips are sold in ten stem bunches, you have to have a perfect crop to get ten bunches. This likely won't happen, so you'll end up with nine bunches and a wasted partial bunch. If you plant a thousand tulips, you'll end up with the same problem, but you'll have 99 bunches that are marketable and just the one leftover bunch. In the first instance you'll have ten percent waste, in the latter just one percent. In this instance, slack is that open space between the marketable and unmarketable flowers, and the big grower has the same amount of slack as the smaller one, but a lower percentage of it and thus a better profitability.

Now take the space in your greenhouse. You order exactly enough plants to fill it since you don't want to waste heat and want to maximize your profits, but your plug producer sends you a tray or two less than you ordered. Your unplanted space is slack, so to avoid that problem either you order too many plants (and face the possibility of encountering a different sort of slack if the plants you ordered do indeed show up) or have an alternative plan, such as planting something that grows quickly from seed.

You'll find slack when you have a row of one length but only need to plant half of it. Do you plant more than you need, do you plant a different species with similar needs, or leave the rest of the row empty? You'll need a feel for slack and the readiness to deal with it. Slack shows up everywhere.

You'll see slack on the delivery van when you don't have enough of one flower variety to fill a bucket—do you mix the bucket with another flower or leave it partially full? If you have round buckets instead of rectangular Proconas, your slack will be where the round buckets don't meet, leaving unused space on your truck that's wasted (when farmers use "circles" for irrigation they lose 28 acres of a 160 acre plot). This means you've not taken advantage of your vehicle and the fuel you put into it. Your profits will suffer accordingly.

Slack abounds in your growing and marketing plan. Specialty cut flowers are called so because they have a short bloom window and brief marketability. Consequently, large suppliers of flowers don't carry these species because customers may take a week to become familiar with them, another to try them, and by the time they decide they love them find they've finished blooming. That's not much slack.

Since the market and growing windows lack much natural slack you have to create it by planting in greenhouse and shadehouses and using techniques that lengthen the season (detailed in Part Two of this book), or you can to move slack into production by planting enough to make early and late harvest larger (and mid-harvest too large) so supply is sufficient to wow your customers for a longer period. There's a bell curve for any species describing its rate of bloom, with a small percentage of plants blooming at the beginning of the season, a small percentage blooming at the end, and the bulk of production coming smack dab in the middle of the curve. Most tulip cultivars, for instance, have a ten day bloom period from first stem cut to last, while many perennials have three weeks from beginning to end. We push the slack to the middle when planting an inexpensive species like Rudbeckia, planting two and three times more than is necessary since we prefer to sell more on the early and late ends of the season at the expense of having too much in its middle. Though this tack works for cheaply grown flowers, it may be inappropriate for more expensive ones.

A cooler creates slack that cut flowers lack by slowing their senescence, giving you time to sell them you wouldn't otherwise have.

Buying land may give you slack that renting does not, since landlords control your decisions, but if buying land so financially straps you that it removes slack from your operation then doing so works against your better interests. Sometimes you want more slack, sometimes you want less, but you always want to make decisions that maintain options, increase freedom, give room for mistakes and room to correct them.

WINDOWS

Scientists and artists alike use windows as a metaphor to describe the space between particular times. There's a window in human development during which syntax can develop, after which a wolf-child might be taught to use words but not to use them with proper sentence structure. There's a window when kittens develop sight during which their vision can be altered so they can't see horizontal lines, and these experimentally changed animals can't be re-taught to see properly at a later date. "The time for taking tarts is when tarts is passing," a friend of ours relates, the wisdom carried down from her Irish ancestors for hundreds of years.

A lot of windows exist in the flower farm world. The window when tillage is proper, the soil neither too wet nor too dry (you can get away with too dry, but not too wet), a window that pops up, then closes, then pops up and closes again all summer as moisture ebbs and flows according not just to your irrigation schedule but weather patterns. The window when to cut a particular flower—better get those delicate flowers cut early or you'll lose today's crop, while sturdier varieties are more forgiving about when in the day they are cut but less so regarding the stage you do so.

There's a window when you need to order next year's plugs and seeds, coming much earlier than intuition might tell you. As soon as you finish harvesting tulips, for instance, it's time to order next year's crop. Wait two months and you'll likely to lose not just your choice of variety but any shipment at all. The same goes for ranunculus and anemones. And plug producers often need at least ten or twelve weeks to grow your plugs from seed to your shipment date.

If you overwinter tulips, other bulbs or plants in a greenhouse or hoophouse, the window for irrigation narrows considerably in the dead of winter. Though plants grow minimally when the ground lies cold, they still require water, so every three or four weeks the driplines need to be turned on to quench the thirst of the drying soil. From about mid-December to mid-January temperatures often dip so low here that lines and filters freeze even in the houses, and only a sunny day thaws them out enough for the two or three hour irrigation period. If no sunny period comes, no watering is possible.

Weather windows lurk near the time of the last spring frost and near the first one as fall approaches. Plugs grown in a greenhouse's ideal conditions can't survive the sudden hard frosts of spring, so you need to order plants to arrive in the window of unlikely frost. By scheduling arrival for ten days before the average last frost, you can catch that window, but watch the forecasts closely and plant only if three or four frost-free nights lie ahead. You may still get caught by frosts. But if you plant late you face the other side of that window where high temperatures make babied transplants wilt and die.

Marketing windows surround holidays, and you may plan to fit harvests into them and fail when the weather turns aberrant. Each species has a harvest window when results are best, some far wider and forgiving than others and all of them shifting in accordance with temperatures.

Be aware that your farm, and any living entity on your farm, has windows of varying sizes that open and close, pertaining to different qualities and needs, to too much or too little, too high or too low—get a feel for the openings they present you and assimilate them to give you the greatest advantage.

SCALE

You can go out and plant forty acres of snapdragons, calculating that at seven or eight stems a plant, eighty cents a stem, and two plants a square foot you'll be rich by the end of the summer, or you can plant ten tulip bulbs, ten sunflowers and ten zinnias, keeping your efforts small but your chance of success high, but neither extreme is very helpful. Somewhere in between lies the scale of your operation—determining that can be difficult if you're just beginning, because how do you know how many clients you will have or how much you can sell to them?

There is no answer unless you call a psychic hotline, so you need to give up that gnawing urge for certainty. Instead, do your homework and make a couple rough estimates, one on the very low side and one on the very high, then pick a spot in the middle that conforms to other factors in your operation.

If you order cut flower plugs, your lower threshold is partially given, since a tray of any plant comes in fixed increments determined by automation. You can't get six, seven or even forty-two plants, instead they come in 32s, 125s, 200s, 392s or other sizes, with annuals rarely sold in smaller amounts than 125. All these come in the same tray dimensions you see at a retail nursery, with higher number trays having smaller plants. If you have greenhouses, your fixed space allows you to find at least an upper limit to your needs—you can only plant about 4000 plants at six inch spacing in a 96 x 20 house, with a thousand in each of four separate "lands" that leave pretty narrow walkways that require slender workers (we actually squeeze in a row of sweet peas between the two middle lands, making for a very tight squeeze).

Determining amounts to plant becomes more difficult on larger plots of land that make you provide your own limits. I still, after all these years, often intend to plant only half a tray of a less marketable species, then at the last moment in a frenzy of wishful thinking and too much coffee plant all the plugs—only to leave half or more unharvested come bloom time. But while planting too much results in waste, planting too little can actually be more of a waste since insufficient numbers of blooms for sale mean clients may go elsewhere to purchase them.

We make about fifty thousand dollars in sales per acre but thirty might be more reasonable to expect, so consider the number of clients you might have and multiply that by weeks of sales and again by what you think you might sell them on average, and you have a ballpark figure of how much land you'll need to plant. Then make a list of species you intend to grow—I start by going through catalogs and marking every single species offered that works as a cut and grows in my area, then work through that list at a later date, striking out the wishful and unlikely until I have a manageable number. Then break up the land into portions appropriate for each: big sellers get more land, smaller ones get less, but even this needs to be tempered since size doesn't determine price—a small bucket of sweet peas brings far more money than a large bucket of sunflowers.

Scale comes into play elsewhere in the business, too. There's no point having too big a tractor for your needs. The irrigation pump should fit the property, too, and the cooler you buy needs to be of such size as to keep a week's worth of sales on hand—we were able to move a hundred and forty thousand dollars worth of product in five months with just a ten by twelve cooler, but I'd recommend buying more space than you need as a crammed cooler can be troublesome in terms of flower retrieval, disease pressure and increased moisture.

You'll learn to use scale when planting and marketing, the two going hand in hand. Designer demand dictates how much you plant, but unfortunately you don't know how much demand there is until you have it on hand! Every bucket route will have a different demand scale running from most marketable flower to least, and even that scale will change, depending on who runs the route.

Our big sellers start with tulips, but that is somewhat an aberration since about a thousand stems a week go to two independent grocery stores. Most clients take only two or three hundred a week, even near holidays. Peonies are the next big seller, racing out the cooler for June weddings. Sunflowers take over in mid-summer. The demand for foliage, we only recently discovered (though we were told this when we started the operation but didn't know what we might grow), rivals demand for focal flowers, with very large orders coming in weekly for Dusty Miller, Sage, Bells of Ireland and anything at all that works as foliage. Clients use Matricaria on a regular basis, making it a top tier flower, too.

The second tier of flowers with steady demand includes snapdragons, Baptisia, Heliopsis, Scabiosa, Icelandic Poppies, Lysimachia, Veronica, and others listed in Part Two of this book, with a number of lesser demand flowers listed there, too. You might think flowers that don't sell well might be flowers to eliminate from production, but the availability of unusual items keeps clients curious about your offerings and gives you the reputation as a supplier of unusual flowers unavailable elsewhere. You want to keep them thinking about you.

You'll never find the perfect plan to fit your scale, mainly because conditions change in a non-static world. One year you'll plant too much so you'll scale back on that species, and then find you've planted too little because market demand changes. Your cooler will have too much empty space early in the year, and not enough room at peak production. But if you factor in upper and lower thresholds for your needs and aim for the middle with your decisions, you've made the best plan you can, just not the perfect one.

TESTING THE WATERS

Whether you're a baby chick pecking its way out through an eggshell or an infant putting every object in its mouth, as a living creature you just naturally test the world—you poke the bear to see if it pokes back, and if it does and you're smart you'll quit poking it; but if it doesn't poke back it might not be a bear, so maybe it's useful in some way. As long as you live, then, you'll never get past Research and Development—you'll always want to try something new. But rather than jumping in whole hog by planting an acre of Tweedia, buy a dozen plants and test them out in those slack places in the greenhouse, or in your home garden.

For annuals, the research task is easy, since they're usually cheap and you get feedback the same season you plant them. You may have to try an annual a second or even third season as you manipulate the conditions—maybe you overwatered the first go round, maybe insects got to them, maybe you grew the wrong cultivar, planted at the wrong time, chose the wrong color—but you know fairly soon whether that flower matches your farm and your clients.

Because perennials often take two years from planting to bloom, feedback from your clients comes slowly and it takes that same time to discern how well they perform in your climate and conditions. We tried bush-type Clematis Integrifolia and didn't get a reading on it until the second year, when we found designers liked the flowers somewhat and the swirled seed heads even more. So we planted a flat of three different colors the next year, this time enough to give a WOW effect when clients see full buckets on the van (too small an amount of any flower sometimes gets lost in the sea of color). It won't be until the fourth year from original test drive that we actually get into full production. By then, who knows, the tastes may have changed.

Slow growing shrubs are even more difficult to assess than perennials. Sometimes it takes many years to discover their worth, as they take valuable space and equally valuable time and effort. We've grown a lot of clunkers—Snowball Spiraea barely lives in our soil; Viburnum Blue Muffin doesn't fruit; Symphoricarpos fruits too late for our market, Indian Currant blooms even later; Crabapples bloom too quickly, hitting our market when it hasn't yet boomed, and the fruit comes on too late, again, for our market; some Hydrangeas don't survive here, Double Flowering Almond may be beautiful and prolific but it shatters and comes too early; Callicarpa grows just fine but doesn't have a long enough season to actually fruit in our climate. The list may be longer, but it's depressing me thinking about the years wasted on these mistakes.

If you're hooked on flowers, there are a number of things you'd like to try, all rolling around in your head, sometimes for years, the pros and cons of trying them out fighting like angels and devils, neither side winning. Tulips were one of those for us, we didn't think something so common and easy to grow would be popular. But after years of skepticism we decided to try just a few so planted two thousand bulbs the first year—a number we could afford, and just enough to test the market and see how much demand they might generate.

They sold out so quickly we doubled the planting the next year, then doubled again the next and just kept raising the number until we maxed out greenhouse space. We likely could sell a hundred thousand a year were we to snag a chain supermarket, as tulips claim a place as a staple for almost anyone who likes flowers.

Make hypotheses, then test them in the real world. If a plant grows too short, try it under shade, if it doesn't sell when you cut it in bud, try cutting in full bloom, if one cultivar of a species doesn't work, it doesn't mean another might not—the list of possibilities goes on forever, and no doubt you're full of questions so just go out and answer them. You don't succeed—or fail— unless you try, so just remember what you learn. You'll never quit fretting about whether something will work or not, so just stop paying attention to that worry and try it.

EMPLOYEES (I SAW YOU SHUDDER)

Thomas Jefferson described slavery as "holding a wolf by the ears" and having employees can feel much the same—you may not really want them but they may be necessary. Maybe you're an employee now and are itching to be the boss, but you may find that being an employer can be as trying as being an employee.

If you're like most employers that I've heard complaining over the years, you want help that can A) do the necessary tasks as well or better than you can, and B) do those tasks for less money than you would. Well, give that up right now—if there were such a person, they'd be in business doing what you intend to do, and doing it better. Flower farming has a unique set of skills and you'll likely find prospects that either know flowers but don't know how to work at the speed and intensity you require or can work hard and fast but don't know flowers. What you're looking for is someone with a master's degree in horticulture but values and knows hard work—dream on.

Small farms, like small businesses, find themselves in a no man's land of needing help but not having enough

74

work to draw skilled laborers. You probably only need someone seasonally, and maybe only part-time, and the farm's tasks are many but last for short periods of time. That makes it difficult to train people, even those who are quick on their feet and make changes easily. It's a tough niche to fill.

Unless you're fortunate, you're going to have to settle for someone unskilled, maybe even someone who's not yet entered the work force. Or you'll have to pull from the pool of romantics who envision the job as prancing through a field with a basket gathering flowers. If you can find someone who's worked in a restaurant and knows how to work fast, work with others, and think on the fly, you might have found a good flower farm worker. Otherwise, you'll have your best luck finding help by networking—if you go to church or have lots of friends, keep an eye out for someone who exhibits the traits you seek. One of our best employees was a local barista we saw working hard and who had great people skills. Another was the daughter of friends who'd grown up on a small ranch. Our most unfortunate hires have been those we advertised for through Craigslist or State Services. You never know who'll show up—we had an older fellow do our weeding one year who had a PhD in English and who'd just published a book critiquing the philosophy of Martin Heidegger.

Simplify tasks for employees, if possible. Designate areas of responsibility. Going over the same acre and doing the same task allows a worker to take ownership and alleviates extra training on your part. Weeding the same plot is self-correcting—the weeder sees what she's missed and hopefully won't miss it again. By her second year our driver knew the clients, knew the routes and traffic patterns, knew the drill. She emptied buckets, restocked, and had two vans ready to go while Jeriann finalized the paperwork for every sale. The knowledge she's assimilated makes her worth twice minimum wage and we pay her accordingly, easing Jeriann's workload in a way that frees us of worry. We know she's going to get things done, and get things done right. We can send her on a drop off delivery and attend to the rest of our business.

Likewise, when we've been able to hire a person to weed on a regular basis, the results, while not perfect, allow that task to be stricken off the list of things to be done. Lining out the day for someone may not take much time, but it breaks up the flow of your day, so having someone dependable show up and start working without oversight frees you from one more headache.

The tasks are so numerous on a flower farm that it's impossible to train someone in a short time. If you're a born teacher, the transfer of knowledge to your employees may come easy. If you're born exasperated, as I was, you may throw up your hands and say "I'll just do it myself". You'll discover a lot about people, you'll discover much about yourself, and hopefully you'll come away with a little humor and irony rather than exasperation.

Part Two

THE BINDWEED HANDBOOK

INTRODUCTION

Once you've decided to start farming, there'll be choices enough to make you crazy, so just keep it simple. There's too many variations and possibilities for anyone to tell you what to do (remember, if it was knowable, it would be risk, not uncertainty, and the latter is where you make money), and any choice you make will have a negative outcome of some sort—it's a bit like parenting: you teach your child tenacity and it turns into stubbornness. Just go ahead, do your best, don't worry, and don't regret.

A few tips in this section would have served me well had I known them as the need arose, so I'll pass them on hoping to save you time and trouble along your learning curve. I'll give you some broad overviews that might clear up some uncertainties about the flower business, and later provide some more specific information on what works for us on our farm. You'll find even more specific info, the real useful stuff, in Armitage's and Laushmann's book, as well as Greer's and Dole's.

In Chapters 2-6, we give you some of the ins and outs of flower farming here in a cold climate, while in Chapters 7-12 we elaborate more detailed information, species by species, on how our techniques work (or don't).

HARVESTING AND PROCESSING

Cutting flowers—simple enough, right? Well, maybe yes, maybe no. Not every flowering species works as a cut, and for those that do timing is crucial, with each species requiring a different stage of cutting and that same timing sometimes adjustable according to where one's market is—our customers want their flowers ready to use when they get them, which means harvesting at the last possible moment, while wholesalers want their flowers to hold through the delivery chain so want you to harvest as early as possible, often in bud.

There's a method to cutting flowers summed up best by the Zen saying "choosing is a sickness of the mind". Spending a lot of time choosing which flower to pick slows you down, and while your primary aim is quality, quantity pays the bills. You need to have a range in your mind ahead of time that spans too open and too closed, and as you move down a row of flowers collect only those that fall into that marketable range. Having this range beforehand means choosing just once, makes further choosing unnecessary, freeing you from taking each bloom and eyeing it at different angles, looking for deformities, measuring openness, judging color. You come to know what to cut and keep, what to cut and discard, allowing you to whip through harvest at three or four times the speed of someone trying to be perfect—someone CHOOSING. This isn't shopping or browsing, it'd deciding and buying.

Be ruthless. If you accidentally deadhead a good flower or leave one, the cost is still much lower than wasting time making sure you don't miss a stem, or worse, cutting bad stems that end up at the designer's shop to mar your reputation—for a buyer always remember the bad stem, the frozen stem, the buggy stem, and you want to be thought of as the source of perfect flowers.

You always want to deadhead flowers too far gone to use, and while you're at it cut any deformed or aborted heads, too. Leaving them today makes tomorrow's job more difficult for sheer mathematical reasons: if you leave a blown flower uncut you'll have to face it the next day and it will crowd your decision about what to cut. Each day you don't deadhead means more unmarketable flowers to crowd your attention, and as the cutting season progresses it becomes more difficult to separate usable from unusable stems, slowing your cutting speed. This is most pressing for fast blooming species like Cosmos and Scabiosa, which can move from tight bud to unusable in the span of a single hot day.

Deadheading is also important in order to funnel the plant's energy away from making seed toward making more blooms, and even more important to undertake on prolific seeders that plant themselves and become weedy in subsequent years.

When you arrange your morning cut start with the most sensitive to heat and wilt. Monarda, Asclepias, and Yarrow are good candidates to start with, while sunflowers and most woodies (other than Physocarpos and Lilacs, which perform better when cut early) can wait. If you cut in the dark, white flowers show up even in moonlight, without a headlamp, while grasses and other bunch-cut crops like sage are easy to harvest in dark conditions if you remember from yesterday's assessment that they're ready. Cut any species that hold dew, which makes them prone to mold in the cooler, after moisture has evaporated, or if you feel you must cut put fans on the harvest in a shaded process area until they're dry. Peonies should be dry before cutting, likewise Lady's Mantle and Bells of Ireland. Zinnias, later in the year, tend to release the cool night's dew slowly and might need to be cut later, too.

Most flowers, if cut in the bud stage, open after cutting, but exceptions exist in plenty. Zinnias and Asclepias shut down immediately once cut, so what you cut is what the customer gets—harvest accordingly. Peonies open if cut in the bud stage, generally, but the sweet spot of cutting varies considerably between varieties. You may not be comfortable cutting peonies until you've cut a few thousand, and then you'll notice subtle alteration in outer petals, small variations in the hardness of the buds. Coral Charm and most other single or semi-double peonies open if cut when even slightly spongy, while Red Charm, an early double, insists you wait until it feels like a marshmallow. Whites may generally be more forgiving, but we've had Festiva Maximas stricken by slight frosts that refused to open until they became very, very soft, while on other years they open when the first shine appears and they have the firmness of a well-done steak. And even this changes according to the weather at the time. If the days hit the eighty or ninety or even hundred degree point, as they sometimes do here during peony harvest, you might need to cut even the reluctant varieties every two hours, as the heat stored in the stems and bud accelerates opening, while an equivalently timed cut on cool days yields a bud that refuses to open. If in doubt, cut the first couple peonies and put them in a vase in a sunny window to see if they open, then proceed according to the result, adjusting your timing.

Initially, cutting flowers may seem daunting, but you don't need to treat them like babies—they're a lot less delicate than you'd imagine. Learn to not just see flowers but to feel them, for you'll be reaching into foliage canopies to search for the right stem to cut. If you have to look each time you cut a stem, you may as well quit, because it's going to take you too long to harvest, you won't be able to afford yourself. Instead of visually searching for the right stem, grab the head of the flower you wish to cut, put your other hand into the canopy in the general area where you think the stem to be, and when you touch the correct stem the blossom hand will feel it move and tell you to cut. Ninety nine percent of the time you'll get the right stem, though once in a while you'll snap those scissors shut again and again and miss (Zinnias seem to be my nemesis in this regard).

Since I cut almost all our flowers, I really do the jobs of two people. Larger cut flower farms require someone to grade the flowers coming in from the field, but because I grade as I cut we bypass a step in processing. If you can hire cutters whose work you needn't assess, pay them properly since they do the work of two.

I sometimes cut as early as 3 AM, using a headlamp, so by the time someone is in the processing area ten or twelve buckets may be ready to put away. Usually all the processor needs to do is to re-cut when necessary, put each bunch in an appropriate sleeve and make sure bucket space is fully utilized. Flowers that have been in the cooler for a few days may need to be recut, their water changed. For cutting flower bunches, it's essential to have a guillotine-like stem cutter (Google it now and get one, they're less than a hundred dollars and will save you thousands), similar to the paper cutters every school once had. Cutting entire bunches with scissors takes exponentially more time and will ruin your hands.

The cooler may be the most important aspect of a flower operation. It protects your harvest, lengthens your market window, is really the equivalent of your bank—without it, the money's not safe. We lived with an 8' x 12' cooler until we reached $140,000 in sales, but by the day before delivery that cooler was packed and any last minute changes required an acrobat to fetch flowers held at the back. If you use Proconas and utilize 30 inches a side for flowers, the aisle becomes less than three feet wide. If you insist on filling that area, as I did when I had ten thousand tulips come on a week before the holiday I grew them for, you can stack Proconas in the center, but remember that a cooler requires air flow and that any disturbance in the flow may create pockets where freezing might occur. Adjust your thermostat upwards and be aware of air circulation patterns.

We upgraded to an 8' x 20' the following year, but it too gets full too quickly and we're thinking about sizing up again. With flowers going out to clients, flowers being organized for orders, and flowers coming in from the field, the cooler becomes a hectic place. But we know that no matter how large a cooler we buy I'll be inclined to fill it—it's just too tempting not to cut more flowers to put in that empty space.

Packing a cooler requires thinking of slack again. No slack resides in the corners since the walls can't be moved, so if you have a lot of one species pack part of the haul in the corner where it won't get in the way. You'll know where to find it—it's the safe deposit box. Put flowers you expect to move more quickly near the front, others against the walls. Think of a doorway leading to two doorways leading to four—if you block the first doorway, you block all of them; if you block one of the last ones, you only block it.

You can fit 9 Proconas on a six foot long, two foot wide shelf by putting four in the back against the wall, parallel, and five perpendicular to them, overhanging just a bit. A hundred Proconas fit in an 8 by 20 cooler without packing anything into the center aisle. With ten or more bunches of flowers in each, at eight dollars a bunch, that's eight thousand dollars. Bank. When the bulky flowers of late summer come in, that bank shrinks as the cooler gets crowded.

We get pre-orders throughout the week for the coming delivery, and of course only the most organized designers get their orders in early and complete. Slack comes into play again here, since by putting orders together, sealing them up with Proconas and collars (and marking them with colored tape, a different color for each client, clipped to the collars), you can put them in a corner or on a shelf of their own and never have to move them until it comes time to pack the van on delivery morning. Theoretically. When the other orders start dribbling in, in pieces, with some additions coming as texts, some as emails, some by the owner, some by the employees, and changes being made, the order you created can turn to chaos in a short time—usually about the afternoon before delivery day, with the nine PM change coming last (other than the 6 AM email the next morning).

We have non-rusting shelves bought from a restaurant supply house which can be adjusted for different heights, but you won't want to be adjusting very much through the growing season so have at least one wall which has a shelf high enough to allow tall things like sunflowers to fit beneath it, and have a place with several shelves where short flowers like sweet peas, poppies and ranunculus might fit. We leave a shelf about a foot from the top where we lay peonies like cordwood as they're harvested (peonies are the only flower we feel comfortable storing dry).

Packing the van is much like packing the cooler, in that you need to put the last order to be taken out in first, into the spot furthest away from the doors where it won't get in the way. That sounds easy enough, especially if everything's pre-sold, but if you have unsold product then you don't want to put tall things by the doors where they'll keep the customer from seeing smaller things. And you have to put small things near the wheel wells where no Proconas will fit. And you need two or three buckets of one flower but only one of another—or do you, can you guess what the clients will want? No matter how you pack, it never will be perfect—because the delivery day is an expression of uncertainty and you're just going to have to deal with it. Afterwards, you'll know how you should have packed, but that won't be any help the next week when you pack it wrong again.

SEASON EXPANSION

Wherever you farm, season expansion becomes possible through the use of shade to cool temperatures, which slows plants down and makes them taller, or protected, heated houses to increase temperatures and speed growth up. You can bring any climate you want to your farm, given the technology available today—it's just a matter of how much you're willing to spend. If you live on Mercury you may not need the greenhouses and if you live on Pluto you just as well forego shade, but everywhere in between benefits from these two techniques. Using shade, you drop at least a zone and using heat you pick up as many as your pockets allow.

Our philosophy of low input requires us to be extremely efficient, so we skip the use of heat through the coldest weeks of winter when air temperatures may never reach freezing. By February1 we feel confident enough of lengthening days to fire up the greenhouses. Because raising the temperature in a greenhouse even one degree corresponds to an exponential increase in BTU use, we forego the optimum temperatures for growing plants and instead just try to keep them alive through cold nights by setting the thermostats between freezing and 40 degrees. Winter sun warms the houses up to more amenable temperatures during the day. Even as late as February, however, a ten day spell of fifteen below nights often strikes, raising the propane bill.

Tulips planted in the houses in mid-October emerge in late January or early February without any heat at all (in fact, we have to keep the temperatures below fifty by keeping the louvers open), forcing our decision to turn on the heat. While cold temperatures won't kill tulips they will damage the foliage and make it unsightly. Outside tulips emerge about eight weeks later, giving insight to how much heat a grower gains from a couple layers of plastic and minimal heating.

We figure the greenhouse gives us the equivalent of a zone 7 climate, two warmer than our own, and to give us a zone 6 climate we use a rollup, or hoop, house. A rollup lacks heating, has the same two layers of plastic with air between to induce warming but its sides remain up in winter and summer—we let them down only on very cold nights. This in-between house gives us about three weeks head start on equivalent species planted in the open. Tulips in the hoop emerge almost simultaneously as those in the greenhouse but they grow much more slowly.

Rollups can be tricky. For the rollup sides (the plastic attaches to a bar that rolls up to the hip of the house, allowing air flow through the house), we initially used the metal piping sold with the house kit from our supplier, and found that water condensed inside the pipe in the winter, froze and exploded the pipe, leaving jagged holes that damaged the plastic attached to it. We lived with the damaged pipe until it came time to change the plastic, then replaced it with 1½" PVC pipe. When we unrolled this version we discovered that at some point in time—either when I was rolling from one end without help on the other, or when I left the pipe supported only on one end— the PVC actually twisted 180 degrees (as if melted!), breaking connections, twisting wiggle wire channel, and damaging the plastic. So keep both ends supported at all times.

A third option to go along with greenhouses and hoophouses is a shadehouse, a structure without plastic to warm plants but one on which shade cloth is applied to slow plants down. Shadehouses can't really change the air temperature much, but they do keep the soil from warming quite as fast and keep leaf surfaces cooler. The effect of shade on different species varies more than does the application of heat; some perennials, like Phlox, bloom a couple weeks later under shade, while tulip stems elongate when shaded but bloom only a day or two later.

We mostly use shade for plants that like mild climates, and to lengthen the stems of species well-received by designers but which grow short in this high altitude and high light area. A majority of species performs better under shade here, preferring gentle weather changes to harsh ones. Shade keeps morning moisture from dissipating rapidly, leading to increased humidity, and at the same time softens the suns magnifying effect through moisture that browns many flowers. This higher humidity leads to more fungal problems, particularly since later blooming coincides with longer nights of more moisture.

We would use shade more extensively if we needed more income, since it ameliorates the harsh climate here. As it is, we grow a 90 x 3 foot plot of Lysimachia Firecracker on one side of a 30 x 96 house, an equal size plot of Gooseneck Loosestrife on the opposite side, a thousand Icelandic poppies in between, with the rest filled with sweet peas or my latest whim. Over the years we've had good crops of Monkshood, Campanula Glomerata, Phlox, Snapdragons, Lobelia, and Berggarden Sage, and bad ones of Lisianthus (the increased humidity created conditions for botrytis), Lavatera, Godetia and Nigella (the three crops grew too tall and lanky).

The same virtues that add heat to our climate in the spring become vices when temperatures rise. One hundred degree temperatures often occur in the houses on a sunny April day and since most species temporarily shut down at ninety, and some species actually go dormant at temperatures even lower than that, we apply shade cloth over the plastic to keep heat at a minimum, at the same time creating conditions for stems to lengthen. The shade keeps wet leaves from searing in the hot sun, too.

If you live in an area of snowfall, greenhouses present a set of problems not suffered by those in the tropics. Dramatic weather swings might mean you put the shade cloth on your houses early to cool them down, then suddenly a late spring snow—the heavy, wet kind—comes and you need to pull those cloths off since they don't shed snow. This happened to us when eighteen inches of heavy snow fell on a late April day. Luckily, we could pull the shade cloth off when we realized the snow wasn't stopping, and on following springs we waited to apply shade.

On a shade house the snow problem worsens since no plastic lies beneath the shade to support it. Much lighter snowfalls of even a couple inches may damage the cloth as it sags beneath the weight. We try to wait until mid May to apply shade, but even then expect to run into problems from time to time and so watch it closely.

Heavy snows may tax the holding capacity for greenhouse structures, so when you buy one make sure they're engineered for your area, and even then, if you're cautious like us, you'll want to help the houses shed their load (if you have gambrel type houses, rather than Quonset, you may not need to help). We do so with a push broom attached to a telescoping paint roller handle. Sold at your hardware store, they'll reach to the eight foot peak of a twenty foot wide house. Anytime the snowload reaches four inches I start to worry, so I drag the snow off despite knowing that the houses can hold that much. Why? Well, if the snow melts and then freezes a crust develops that roughens the plastic surface. The snow then tends to sit, rather than slide off, as temperatures warm, so further snows collect and increase the snowload. Pulling the snow off is just another insurance policy. The extra work might be unnecessary but seems better than suffering the consequences of a collapsed house.

Most houses that collapse do so when wind drives snow and deposits drifts on one side, giving that side a snowload much, much heavier than on its counterpart. Arch designs depend on the sides working together, one protecting the opposite, sharing the load, so when one side does all the work, the arch loses its carrying capacity. For that reason, a three inch snowfall combined with a thirty mile wind that creates drifts can be worse than a soft one foot snowfall that evenly distributes.

SEEDING AND PLANTING

Because planting plugs provides a head start on weeds we prefer doing so to direct seeding, but a few species grow so quickly and easily that we do break out the Earthway seeder from time to time. Local farmers no doubt laugh when they see me behind a two wheeled seeder, but our hundred dollar planter costs fifty or sixty thousand dollars less than theirs—and that two hundred foot row nets more cash than five acres on their farms. You can plant an acre with the Earthway in an hour or two (we rarely plant more than a half-mile of row at a time, though). It suffices for us.

If you're a machine guy, though, there are more expensive and accurate implements to attach to the tractor. These generally have a better selection of seed plates, the lack of which can be a problem with the Earthway. Seeds that don't match up with its plates' premade holes either get planted too thinly or thickly, so we err toward the latter—you can thin out a too heavily planted row but you can't magic a thicker stand of flowers. The odd shapes of some flower and grass seeds can be a problem, too, and again we choose to plant seeds like Zinnias and Cosmos, which are light and thin and long, thickly and either let them thin themselves or thin them at the first cultivation. And tiny seed that the Earthway might plant if we could only afford enough to fill the hopper (given the price of some species, that might run in the thousands of dollars) gets an inaccurate, sloppy hand-sow. Usually such small seed requires surface sowing, so to give good soil contact I use a very expensive tool made especially for such action—my feet, carefully placed to compress the seed into the earth.

Early crops we sow as soon as the ground can be worked include Larkspur, Dill, Bupleurum, Lepidium, Clarkia, and Atriplex. Larkspur and Bupleurum often perform best when seeded in late fall but we're too tired when the window for that planting rolls around, so they generally get planted in the spring. We often forego Bupleurum, since it blooms simultaneously with Lady's Mantle, a perennial with the same color palette (our clients often confuse the two species), and because it often succumbs to a soil disease here. Because it self seeds, we still cut a few bunches from random plants scattered through the field.

The moment ground temperatures reach fifty degrees we sow the first crop of sunflowers, one of our biggest sellers. We plant double the area we seed on subsequent sows because early season hunger for suns is strong, and also because growth in May and April is considerably slower than in July or August, when days are much longer. If ground temperatures warm early, emerged seedlings may face a late frost. Though even hard frosts rarely kill them they will act as if they've been pinched and produce three or more stems with smaller flowers that make them unusable for our market. Consequently, when that frost threat comes we just rake or shovel a small amount of dirt over the seedlings to protect them for a night or two, after which they'll push through the soil and continue to grow unscathed.

Growers who live where the killdeer—an annoying, robin-sized bird that never sleeps or stops moving—is indigenous may need to cover their sunflower plantings, as these birds somehow locate the seeds and pull them from the soil, sometimes decimating a crop. When you see a hole every six inches and the open hulls of a sunflower seed, you'll know you need to put a layer of ground cloth over the soil until seeds are germinated. Killdeer occasionally go for broom corn and even zinnias, and are notorious for liking squash and other large vegetable seed.

After the early sunflower planting we wait three to four weeks before sowing the succeeding, smaller crop, after which we plant every seven days to give us continual harvest. With erratic weather the early crops sometimes squeeze together, and occasionally a later planted crop will bloom before one planted earlier.

We have no luck with the vase life of multi-branched varieties, though we do grow a row of Sungold, a teddy bear type that lasts well. Sungold, a long season variety that takes ninety days from sowing to bloom, also serves as a shade break for a sweet pea crop. We plant single stem Vincents, finding their size and form the most desirable to our clients. A short season crop, they beat our old favorite Sunbright by 10 days and their stem diameter measures much smaller, thus making them more usable as well as more manageable in the cooler and the van. If you want a real big stem, grow the short season variety Full Sun in the summer, as we did, and sell the stalks as firewood or table legs. Their one-inch diameter stalks were a drawback that overwhelmed their good features, a fine form and a very large head, perhaps because they're bred for winter production in warmer climates.

We like to have a green or yellow center sunflower on hand for more edgy designers, and though we can sell up to half as many as dark center we now sometimes forego planting them, as the only variety (Sunbeam) we found over the years that resisted head-distorting insects no long shows up on the market. Rather than fight the insects (which avoid, for the most part, their dark center counterparts) with constant spraying, we plant a mini sunflower with a yellow-green center, Peach Passion, which despite its floppy stem has a good following.

Zinnias are another fast grower that seeds easily. Wait until the ground temperature hits 60 degrees (about the first of June here) because earlier planted seed just rots. We plant thickly and while other sources may direct you to thin zinnias out, we find they do just fine thinning themselves. Once in a while we seed a subsequent crop of zinnias a couple weeks later as a heavily harvested plot can get a bit ratty and diseased.

Orlaya, a Queen Anne's lookalike without the height but with a better vase life, germinates in cooler temperatures so can be planted even before the last frost date. While it blooms continuously after cutting each subsequent harvest becomes more difficult, so seed another crop a month later, and possible another one after that. Though it tends to be short here, designers love this crop and buy in large amounts. Harvest before pollen shows.

We sometimes direct seed Celosia though it often performs poorly in our climate. Too much light in the day results in shorter stems than growers in warmer climates get, while our humid nights as harvest nears combines with an early morning hot sun to create unsightly stains and unmarketability. Only Pampas Plume, a cheap seed that mixes fuschia, gold, green and some odds and ends of varying shades of red, and Sylphid grows well for us on a consistent basis.

Grasses, easy to germinate and predictable, provide a staple for our clients. We direct seed almost all of ours, though we buy plugs of Chasmanthium (Northern Sea Oats) every two or three years, which, while perennial, tends to die out due to heavy cutting and cold winters. We also use plugs of Briza Maxima, Quaking Grass (our clients call it "snake grass" because its heads mimic a rattlesnake's rattles), because a seeded crop hasn't enough time in our area to get a proper stem length before it blooms. Other perennial grasses better grown from plugs may be the Switchgrasses, Miscanthus, Sorghastrum, and Ravennae grass. Melica, an early flowering perennial grass, comes easily from seed but cheap plugs are a better route to take. Cut back Melica after harvest for a second cut four or five weeks later, and cut again if you want yet another harvest late in the year.

Annual grasses we've tried and eliminated from our list include Canary Grass (its erratic pollen shed makes it difficult to cut in a proper stage), Limelight Millet (aphids here love it almost more than anything else), and Tapestry Millet (its form resembles the more easily grown Highlander enough that one makes the other redundant). We direct seed Foxtail Millet, the earliest to germinate and so plantable near the last frost date, through the summer, spacing three to four weeks between plantings early, when the temperatures are low, then seeding every two weeks clear through July for continuous harvest. Highlander Millet we treat similarly, though its higher germination temperature calls for a first planting later by two weeks, and its longer harvest window means we can widen the time between seedings. Its period from seed to bloom, being much longer than Foxtail Millet's, means our last seeding comes around the first of July as later plantings won't come to fruition.

All the direct seeded crops get planted above two rows of drip tape we lay beneath the soil surface. The two rows rest eighteen inches apart (the distance chosen to fit in the center of our tractor's wheelbase) and two to four inches deep, and provide a mark for the Earthway seeder to follow. We always lay tape immediately before planting, as burying it too far ahead of time makes it possible for ill-timed rains to harden the soil, making seeding impossible.

Small plugs (200s) fits best to the drip tape method of planting, as being finger-sized they're just right to fit in the hole made by that inexpensive tool, the index finger. If you're swift and deft, you just grab a plug with the finger and thumb one hand, push a hole in the soil with a finger from the other hand, put the plug in the hole as you pull the finger out, the "shoulders" of the plug always slightly deeper than the soil, as the soil will sink after irrigation. If you're a real stickler, firm up the soil around each plug, but only in extremely dry soil do I take such extra steps.

Larger plugs require a minor amount of digging, and will require closer watching for two reasons: being more mature plants, and being planted in more medium than smaller plugs, they use more water. The total surface area that contacts your soil multiplies manifold, and that's the crucial area that must be breached by both water and root before you have to quit worrying about plugs. Until the roots from the babied transplants foray out into the farm soil, a gap of air remains that quickly dries the plug. Be watchful, especially with large plugs—we water every other day for a week or even two.

Before planting, examine the plug roots. Trim root-bound plugs, those that circle the bottom of the plug multiple times, sometimes leaving no soil exposed. Matricaria and Blackeyed Susans rarely come without their roots requiring a snip of the scissors—don't be afraid to lop off a quarter or even a half inch of root.

Bare root stock, being much larger than plugs, requires a change in planting method when using drip tape. Using the widest possible "shovel" or furrower you can get for your tool bar, make a ditch 8-10 inches deep, then lay a drip line in the bottom, place bare roots like Phlox or Eremerus on the tape, in the furrow, at the desired spacing and depth, then cover by hand or with a rake. We sometimes use the drip layer, too, and very carefully make the same furrow between the two lines, thereafter providing water from both sides of the row, rather than from just beneath. Always researching, we planted our last peonies this way, hoping a watering from each side rather than from directly under the root would inhibit rot and disease. We normally plant peonies in a deep furrow with in-tubing emitters directly beneath the root, as lines aboveground constantly shift with air temperatures and emitters consequently sometimes end up far from the plant.

GROWING IN CRATES

Most bulbs and some bare roots come in plastic crates, eighteen inches wide and twenty four long, six to eight inches tall. Though porous enough to allow air and water passage through their walls, they are quite sturdy and built for easy handling and stacking. You may see something similar in large grocery stores in the produce section, or a smaller version in the dairy area. Over the years, a grower can amass a great number of these—we accumulate fifty or more a year, since we grow about twenty five thousand tulips, five hundred coming in a crate.

Many growers use the empty crates to grow lilies and tulips and other bulbs, but they can be used for just about any crop you'd like to be able to move from place to place. Typically, you lay a sheet of newspaper on the bottom of the crate to create a surface, fill it with a couple inches of growing medium and fertilizer, place bulbs or bare roots at an appropriate spacing, then fill the crate with more potting soil. The crates can then be placed in a row with a couple lines of drip tape tied to the crates on top for irrigation.

Most growers do this above ground, but we find that the sides of the crates lose moisture more quickly than the centers, more surface being exposed to the elements, so bulbs planted at the edges don't perform as well. So we dig a shallow trench in which we place the crates with their tops relatively level with the ground, the lessened evaporation rates and exposure to both cold and hot temperatures giving crops a more even growth pattern.

Growing tulips in crates allows them to be more easily discarded or even re-used than they would be if grown in the ground. You can just lift the crates from the trench, overturn them and sort the bulbs from the medium. We give the discarded bulbs to local charities—prisons, parks, highway projects—that always enjoy freebies. If you plant bulbs in the ground you have to dig them up with a shovel or fork. You may manage to retrieve the main bulb, but most bulbs form offspring (bulblets) that detach when disturbed, thus evading your scrutiny and remaining to become weeds for years to come.

The crates allow for easy "transplanting". We plant a new crop of daffodils each year in crates in the rollup hoophouse, giving us an additional product to sell with tulips on early routes. Daffodils don't command the price that tulips do, though the bulbs are equivalently priced or even more expensive, but unlike tulips they produce stems year after year so needn't be discarded. It takes a couple seasons to make a profit from Narcissus, so we move the inside daffodil crates (completely intact), once they're harvested, into an outside trench where they'll bloom the next year, but at a later date, just after the next new crop is finished blooming in the hoophouse (we don't plant Narcissus in the greenhouse, since they bloom a couple weeks before the tulips that initiate the beginning of our sales route).

We sometimes plant bulb crops not hardy to our zone in crates in the hoophouse, where they pick up another climate zone. Brodiae, hardy only to zone 6, grows fine through the winter in our hoophouse but its tiny bulbs and their bulblets become too weedy to plant in the ground. Some Ornithogalums, Ranunculus and Anemones can likewise be planted in crates in protected areas and are then easily removed in the spring to allow a quick second greenhouse crop of another species.

WEEDING

In terms of cost, weeding approaches and perhaps exceeds that of harvesting, depending on how much weed pressure your crops suffer. Eliminate, whenever possible, weed habitat by keeping surfaces dry if you live in a desert-type climate and covering them with mulch if in wetter areas. Many perennials, like Asclepias, Clematis and Baptisia, tolerate deep mulch that eliminate settings for weeds, and even annuals, once established, can be covered by mulch. We find it's essential to mulch woodies that have large canopies which make weeding nearly impossible. This can be done either with plastic weed mat, wood shavings or similar products.

A "dry mulch" works, where possible—by using a scuffle hoe that cuts weeds off just below the surface, the thin, topmost layer of soil is sufficiently disturbed to dry out and prevent seed germination. The scuffle hoe works well on transplants, particularly if your spacing is just a bit wider than the hoe's width—one pass between plants eliminates weeds in the center, and a pass down each side of the plug row with a much faster wheel hoe (also a scuffle type hoe) takes care of the rest, with little hand pulling required. The scuffle only works on smaller weeds, so after the first or second weeding you'll need to switch tools, but in areas without rain very little weeding is necessary once the initial flush of spring weeds is gone.

By planting plugs your desired plants get a head start on weeds, making cultivation easier, so when you figure your operational costs compare the more expensive plugs to not just the same species as cheaper seed, but to the cost of seed plus the costly hours spent weeding them to nurse them to a viable stage. Perennials, taking longer periods of time to germinate and being slower growers, tend to compete poorly with weeds, so the bigger plant you get the less you'll have to weed.

Some crops may not come as plugs, though, and when dealing with these you may be ahead to irrigate and till, irrigate and till the area to be planted to destroy as many weed seedlings as possible before planting. On new land or land taken out of pasture, you may want to spend an entire year tilling under new crops of weeds (always tilling well before weeds bud—many species continue to form seed even if chopped down or sprayed in bud stage) to make subsequent years of farming easier.

The best technique for saving weeding work, hands down, is irrigation through drip tape underground, at root level or deeper, as what water reaches the surface will evaporate in warmer weather. Surface weed seed doesn't have enough moisture and time to germinate.

The drip system doesn't help much on shallowly seeded crops like celosia, however. These need a fairly long period of time in moist soil, resulting in higher weed pressure because surface soil can't be allowed to dry.

A local equipment fabricator engineered our drip tape layer for a couple hundred dollars, and almost any equipment dealer sells the tool bar it attaches to for about the same price. The layer amounts to nothing more than a narrow shank that breaks the soil, behind which attaches, via weld, a flared section of tubing (flared to avoid sharp edges which might damage the drip tape as it flows downward through and out). The tubing, large enough in diameter for the tape to flow freely, guides the tape from a roll set above it on two supports. The supports hold a rod between them to act as an axle for the tape roll. The tape pulls through the tubing, which is rounded off at a ninety degree angle that opens at the level of the shank depth. The shank forms a furrow, the tape immediately flows into it, and gravity does the work of covering the tape with soil falling onto the tape. We adjust the shank to bury the tape three inches deep but it can be laid more deeply, if desired—just remember that water wicks upward somewhat slowly, so shallowly rooted plants may not get their needed water as quickly if the tape sets too deep. If we feel the soil to be too loose, we run a roller filled with water over the tape (we plant two rows between the tractor wheels, eighteen inches apart) to firm it up.

The tape works well with transplants—if you're a real wizard, you can water the day before planting just enough to show wet spots that give the transplanting crew a guide for spacing—but also works for direct seeded crops. You may want to run your seeder just to the side of the tape if you think you need more depth for the roots.

Drip tape distributed above ground is at the mercy of wind and sun. Wind blows empty tape wherever it wishes, requiring you to retrieve and return it when irrigation time comes, and sun lengthens any stretch of tape, creating humps, curves and waves in your once straight line. These perturbations try to return to straightness when night temperatures contract the tape but never return to their original placement. Even a two percent stretching effect by the sun will lengthen a hundred foot length of tape by two feet, and while the two feet would be manageable if the stretch came at the ends of the tape and then returned, it becomes quite a problem when distributed throughout the tape's entire length.

This warping occurs with any flexible plastic tubing, including Netafin and poly pipe with emitters, so be prepared. The back and forth effect on poly can be eliminated when used on shrubbery by starting with a wavelength pattern upon initial planting—lay the tubing on the left of the first shrub, on the right of the second, alternating troughs and crests so that the heating and cooling of days and nights pushes in and pushes out at the humps.

Gathering tape at the end of the year is the biggest drawback of this type of irrigation. It can be a messy procedure. Drip tape remains viable underground for several years, so when used on perennials it needn't be retrieved until the bed dies out, but it needs to be removed from the field when used with annuals in order to allow tillage for the next year's planting. While large farms buy or make retrieval systems that lift and roll used tape, smaller farmers like us have to do it by hand.

To remove tape once you abandon a crop, till the rows with a rotovator—shallowly enough so the tape's not damaged, or you may end up with plastic confetti. Shallow rooted crops often only require a single tillage, but large rooted species like sunflowers may take an initial till, a two or three week period of waiting for root deterioration, then a second or even a repeated wait-and-till before tape can be pulled easily. Once the tape pulls up, you just ball it up into whatever shape you deem easiest to deal with, then discard or recycle. If you have a multi-fuel compatible furnace, the plastic can be used as a fuel source—remember, though, it burns swiftly and very hot.

Species that make retrieval difficult include most perennials, especially rhizomes—and broom corn, an annual, releases the tape only after a winter of frost and thaw.

If you want to speed up the procedure of retrieval, you can build a lifting device that attaches to a tractor hitch. Such a device can be as simple as a blade wide enough not to damage the tape, which when sunk beneath the tape softens the soil so it releases its hold. The lifter is little more than a potato or bulb digger without the chains, so you might find a discarded antique that will suffice, but we had a fabricator in Wyoming make ours for three hundred dollars—antique farm equipment here has all become lawn ornaments for the gentry.

Another drip tape drawback arises when someone cuts a line, typically when weeding. We use a soil knife to dig out troublesome weeds with taproots—like field geranium or dandelions—so if the worker tries to extract a weed growing directly over a buried drip line he may cut the tape when digging too deeply. Mice or voles sometimes gnaw holes in the lines in winter, requiring repair in spring. And occasionally a line may simply quit working, roots having somehow sealed off the passage. In all cases, splicing becomes necessary, and below-ground fixes can be difficult in the same way as below-ground plumbing is, as once the bad segment of the tape is cut out the connector is rarely long enough to fill the resultant space, requiring a double connection with a short piece of inserted tape.

A "hook" hoe, or wire weeder, has a support on just one side and a blade shooting out like an L. We love this hoe for early weeding, its deftness allowing a weeder to get very close to the plant by placing its elbow against the stem. You can also use the hoe's open end to thin thickly planted seeds like Celosia, Clarkia, some grasses and zinnias.

The same tool bar that supports the drip tape shanks can be used to attach "duck feet", V–shaped cultivators that slide beneath the soil surface at the level you wish. We only use these in the tractor wheel tracks, setting them an inch below the soil to cut any weeds off. The duck feet come with wings of all sizes, so depending on how confident you are of your driving, you can get as close to the plants on either side of the row as you wish. If you always plant two rows of plants between the wheels, as we do (18" apart), you can attach a duck foot in the middle of the tool bar as well as behind the wheels, so it weeds between the rows as well as along their sides. There's a pitfall to this cultivating technique that requires nerves of steel: on the one hand, if you look behind you to see how you're doing, you tend to pull the steering wheel one way or the other, causing what farmers here term "cultivator blight"— the rear of the tractor swings the opposite way that you turn, throwing the duck feet into the very plants you're trying to coddle and protect; on the other hand, if you don't look behind you have to trust your driving, hope you aren't ruining the entire planting.

One of my less favorite jobs, I admit.

PERENNIALS

I won't list all the perennials we grow, but these are some of the more important ones on our farm. Many perennials aren't open to season manipulation, being daylength sensitive (well, even these can be altered if you can afford money for lights), but we've tried to extend the season of many and describe the results below.

Alchemilla. Also known as Lady's Mantle, Alchemilla's small, electric yellow bloom sets off its foliage that looks like, well, the lady's mantle you see on Victorian dresses. A long lasting foliage plant, cut as a field bunch, it should be harvested before the tiny blooms starts to brown. It holds well in the cooler, though it dirties its water and needs a change every three or four days, and almost all designers desire it. It blooms after vernalization and we find its harvest difficult to manipulate, though planting some in North-South rows and some in East-West rows spreads the cutting window out another week.

Trim Lady's Mantle back to the nubbins early in the spring to get rid of dead foliage—you need every inch of stem when cutting this short plant in order to give designers more usage. Don't, however, shear it in late summer, as it needs the energy from its remaining foliage to prep for the coming years.

Asclepias. What a species, long lasting in the vase, loved by avant garde and traditional designers alike. The white perennials like Ice Ballet, the pink forms like Cinderella or the orange Tuberosa all strike the florist's fancy. We plant new crops every year as heavy harvesting weakens Asclepias, but sometimes get three or four years from a planting. Tuberosa, unlike the white and pink forms, flowers heavily even the first year, though stems are often short, and plugs planted before the last frost date will begin blooming just as the first crop of prior year's plantings finish. And if you cut back Tuberosa after flowering it will bloom again—just make sure you cut it low to the ground or your stems will be short and unmarketable. In our zone, the white and pink forms bloom the first year only enough to pay back the costs of the plants, and second flushes on older plantings rarely produce significantly.

The annual form, Curassavica or "bloodflower", has less appeal than the perennials, primarily because it's more difficult to keep hydrated. It's also more prone to damage from thrips and it's easy to lose a crop, though if you cut your lost crop back close to the ground you'll find you'll get another flush. In a greenhouse, bloodflower blooms earlier and sports much taller stems that require netting.

Aphids sometimes plague Asclepias. About one year in eight an orange aphid we almost never see on any other plant shows up and panics us, but a quick dose of Malathion or your favorite remedy takes care of them more easily than other aphids are dealt with—they seem not to reproduce as efficiently as green and black aphids.

If you resist heavy harvesting, an Asclepias bed remains viable for many, many years, but because we mow it down after bloom to prevent excess seeding we rarely use a plot for more than three years. Tuberosa seems more vigorous when planted in a "happy place", but in general has a greater mortality for us, being susceptible to soil-borne pathogens.

Baptisia. Along with other early blooming perennials and shrubs, Baptisia responds to a simple manipulation: plant half your crop in north-south rows, half in east-west, the latter blooming ten days to two weeks earlier due to its getting more of the winter sun, which shines from the south, to warm its roots. If you're a year or two away from starting your farm, take soil temperatures in different areas at the same time to show you where your hot spots and cold areas lie, and plant accordingly.

Baptisia comes in many colors, all of them nice, the blue a true blue rarely found in the flower world, where most plants sold as blue turn out to be a shade of purple. In areas where Baptisia grows as a native, growers sell it not just as a flower but as a pod, but our crop gets afflicted by a fungus that leaves the seedheads unattractive. The foliage works for designers needing something different for a filler, but don't cut too much away as Baptisia grows slowly and needs its leaves to invigorate future growth.

Heliopsis. A very vigorous plant (and a water-hog), Heliopsis can be cut back before bloom to delay flowering, or sheared immediately after harvest to induce a late, second bloom. Since it needs no vernalization, you can also plant plugs for a same year flowering that will come two to three weeks after older plants are harvested. It has a long harvest window, though we generally cut it before it's too open since our frequent hot winds tend to burn its petals. The foliage of the variegated form of Heliopsis, though interesting, doesn't hold up in the vase.

Campanula. Glomerata is the only Campanula I'd call a true perennial, and like all Campanulas it's a quirky plant for the cut flower business. The nursery business doesn't seem to be on the same page when it lists cultivars, so you may have to shop around before you find the right one. Superba hit the spot for us, but different suppliers seem to have different genetic material so stick with what works for you, since there are many unacceptably short varieties. Both white and purple sell fairly well, but work better under shade for us, and cutting them can be a challenge if pollinators get to the blooms before you do. Sporting dozens of small blooms on a nearly spherical head, Glomerata look best if cut open for local sales, but early blooms senesce if pollinated, offsetting the attractiveness of new blooms.

Clematis Recta. What a remarkable plant, loved by ahead-of-the-curve designers and old school florists alike, it blooms in late May and June here, and if sheared back will bloom a month later—and then, if sheared back, will bloom again in August! It needs to be staked or netted, and can be cut one stem at a time or cut in field bunches. It's admittedly not a pleasant cut (few flowers that need netted are) until the checks start rolling in to temper one's dismay. We pull the Recta downward through the netting (when you hear tearing foliage, don't panic, the tendrils ripping away don't always cause damage), leaving the netting intact for second and third harvests. Shear right to the ground for the longest future stems.

Clematis Recta Purpurea, with similar blooms but dark foliage much like Lysimachia Firecracker, grows less vigorously but otherwise has almost identical characteristics.

Other clematis we use include Paul Farges, Integrifolia and Ternifolia. Integrifolia, bushy like Recta but shorter, also requires staking, and like Recta grows rapidly so can be harvested multiple times. We cut the flowers on the first crop in May, sometimes a single stem at a time but sometimes as a field bunch, then let the second crop form seed heads that look like spacy swirls. We harvest these as bunches, a simpler procedure than cutting single stems, and find they appeal to almost all designers.

If you don't mind difficult cuts, try Paul Farges, a small flowered species that may grow fifty feet in a season. Its quarter sized, starlike flowers come in multiple numbers along its lengthy stem, which can be harvested and used on arches since it has a long vase life. Being a climber, it possesses tendrils that may tangle the stems but if your designers aren't too fussy they won't mind the difficulties—a flowering vine like this is hard to find. The longer you cut the vine, the more difficult it is to deliver, so keep that in mind when you price it to your clients. Cut back Paul Farges as hard as you want; plant enough to prune at varying lengths and you'll have a crop that lasts all summer long—longer than you probably want it to. And if you figure out a way to train Paul Farges that makes it easily harvestable, patent your system and retire to the Bahamas.

A similar vine that flowers in September, Ternifolia has smaller but nearly identical flowers to Paul Farges but cuts more like Recta.

Delphinium. Using different cultivars of Delphinium will stretch your cutting season, and plugs in 200 trays planted in early May will flower almost immediately after crops planted in prior years, lengthening harvest yet further. Cutting back just-harvested plants will result in the death of some if cut too severely, but those that survive will flower at the end of the summer when Delphiniums from larger companies are scarce. We've tried Delphiniums in greenhouses and hoophouses but disease pressure there seems too great to fight and the stems seem weak in relation to outdoor-grown crops.

The Aurora series blooms evenly with thickly blossomed stems, while Pacific Giants present an airier look, grow taller and more erratically. Lavender Aurora falls off our list this year, having succumbed to disease for two consecutive seasons, but the other colors remain as staples. Guardian series bloom a week earlier for us, not early enough to justify planting them as a season extender, but Pacific Giants bloom a bit later so we sometimes plant a few for a later crop. We don't grow Bellamosum, though clients often ask for it, as we've never been able to avoid the mildew that afflicts it.

Eremerus. Few flowers get someone's attention like Foxtail Lily. We've had cars stop on the highway, the drivers thinking our field on fire when the sun struck it just right. At four, five, even six feet tall, Eremerus fits a market niche smaller than its true appeal, being more suitable for lobbies and big events than for everyday household affairs. Easy to grow, easy to cut, relatively easy to store given its cumbersome stature, commanding a high stem price, and having a long storage life in the cooler as well as the vase, Eremerus deserves a place on any farm. Don't overwater, however, particularly after it goes dormant. Greenhouse grown Eremerus blooms earlier than its outdoor counterparts, but as for any perennial grown in the greenhouse, may not return the profit, inch for inch, that multiple crops of annuals do.

Lysimachia. Another species essential to us for its longevity in the vase and its aesthetic desirability, Lysimachia plays a big part in our sales. We grow two kinds, Firecracker and Gooseneck Loosestrife (not to be confused with the invasive loosestrife), that seem unrelated when looking at them but which must be true siblings, as both are favorites of the root weevil, the only pest which seems to bother them (we've never seen aphids on either form). Firecracker foliage has a dark color similar to Diablo ninebark and blooms mid-season with many small yellow flowers, while Gooseneck has a white flower shaped like a fat Veronica and blooms in mid-July and August. Neither get tall enough for market when we grow them in the field, so we have beds under shade cloth that encourage them to grow at least eighteen inches taller, making netting necessary.

Firecracker grows tall enough to use as foliage as early as mid-May and we have it on the availability list from then until we grow tired of cutting it. The Firecracker we cut early will grow back quickly and provide a second cut (when harvesting, shear right to the ground so the second flush of stems lengthens more). We also cut it in bloom, and though its electric yellow may not fit the color scheme of a designer's particular need the flowers can be easily picked off to leave just the dark foliage. Sometimes, no doubt from fertility causes, Firecracker can present leaves with a pinkish hue that designers love.

Gooseneck, like Firecracker, is a rhizome that fills a bed quickly and throws many stems, and its spiky form makes it valuable in designer work. It blooms for a month or more under shade, and because it's thin and small a lot will fit in a bucket, making it one of the most profitable flowers for us if you calculate by how much space it takes in a truck (compare a bucket of sunflowers at roughly a hundred dollars to an equivalent area for gooseneck at three hundred and fifty). The root weevil that inevitably plague Lysimachias (and Scabiosas and Peonies) can be controlled with the pesticide Tempo by applying it every three weeks from mid–May (or first sign of damage) through the season. A nematode is sold claiming itself a control, as well, but we had no luck when we used it (it could have been the applicator's fault, of course).

A note on root weevil: for years we attributed root weevil damage to other pests, since the bite–like serrations it leaves looks much like grasshopper work. Since root weevils come out at night to do their mischief, you'll only see a few late-to-beds in the morning. Go out with a flashlight a couple hours after sunset, look for a black beetle about three-eighths of an inch long, and you might find the culprit who's been decimating your crop. Root weevil work on Lilac, Osier and Roses, too (funny, they like the same leaves that leafcutter bees do and leave a similar cut pattern).

Monarda. The annual form, Citriodora, can be manipulated by shearing before bloom or doing so afterward for a second flush. The perennial forms are less amenable to the same technique, but plugs planted in May, though they rarely flower the first year for us, will grow to harvestable foliage that has a good vase life. Plants from earlier years often don't have such nice foliage, but flower prolifically in the right setting. You can't exactly stretch out the season of a particular color, but Monarda comes in so many hues that the harvest season may last longer than five weeks. Red comes first for us, never quite early enough to hit the Fourth of July hard, then raspberry, then pink and purple and lastly, white. The white browns easily so must be cut when the first inkling of color appears, but like all Monardas it opens quickly even in the cooler.

Grasshoppers tend to like Monarda, and mildew strikes if grown in a protected area, out of the wind.

Peonies. If you have sufficient resources you can force peonies to come early by growing them under plastic. Early on in our business we devoted an unheated hoophouse to peony production with great success. We paid for the house and roots in a single year with a prolific crop that came three weeks earlier than crops planted outdoors. However, on subsequent years we found that extremely hard frosts damaged the inside peonies despite the double layer of plastic protection, and rather than provide portable heating in the house on those short spells we moved the crop outdoors to use the house for other crops.

If you worry less than I do about heaters overturning and burning down the farm, it might be to your benefit to plant indoors and move your peony crop forward.

A problem for inside peonies not occurring on their outside counterparts is their extreme stickiness—after a harvest of indoor peonies, you'll need to change your clothes (if indeed you can still walk in your sugar-laden pants), as the weather and insects that clean up peony exudations don't help at all under cover. This means you must move the peonies rapidly through the sales chain, as the excess sugars provide perfect habitat for mold formation in the cooler.

Being susceptible to frost at inopportune times, peonies resist forcing outside but by choosing different cultivars having similar colors but differing bloom times you can stretch your availability of whites, reds and pinks over a longer period. Coral Charms and Red Charms are about as early as we get, though the species form "Rubra", a parent of Red Charm, flowers about a week earlier with shorter stems. We've found that later flowering peonies suffer more frost damage than early varieties, defying logic but still nonetheless true for us.

The peony season can be stretched into mid July or even later since the stems hold well (weeks, sometimes months if you dare) in the cooler if you don't put them in water after cutting. When ready to sell them, just pull them from the cooler, cut a couple inches off, and put into water. Watch the stems stored in the cooler closely, though, as any moisture combined with the natural peony sugars inspires mold growth, easily washed off but still requiring time (and thus, money).

Bowl Of Cream is the best white for our customers, though any white at all will do during wedding season, even prolific Festiva Maxima. Scarlet O'Hara is an early, single prolific red, and Cytherea is a later single with a watermelon color that will do when someone wants Coral Charm. We've found that roots from different suppliers perform with varying results, so stick with what works. We've lost entire crops bought from vendors who may be reliable for others but whose roots succumbed to disease while our favorite vendor's didn't.

A new grower squeamish about cash outlay may shy away from planting peonies, since a single root may cost from three to ten dollars and may not yield a single stem for three or four years. But if at all possible, he should do the unthinkable and spend as much as he can stand to on a planting, even if it's just fifty plants a year. He'll be rewarded over time, since a plot may last decades.

Phlox: We plant phlox roots every year, as the first year roots will flower shortly after those planted in prior years (albeit with shorter stems). This lengthens out the harvest period to at least six weeks, and if you have some room in a shaded house you can lengthen cutting time even further. We cut back severely after harvest, hoping for a second cutting, but oftentimes the later stems aren't marketable. Zone six growers in a less light-filled area might have better luck.

We use David for white sales, Blue Paradise for blue, and supplement with Laura. Red and orange varieties seem fussy about our alkaline soil and excess sunlight so fail to thrive outside, so we sometimes grow them in the greenhouse where conditions are more amenable.

Another variety that resists our farm, the white Miss Lingard, blooms earlier than David by a couple weeks and hits the wedding season perfectly.

Phlox is a real moisture hog, so don't short it at bloom time or harvests will suffer badly.

Platycodon. This crop will bloom a second time if cut back immediately after harvest. We find it sensitive to alkaline soil so keep planting it until we find an area on the farm where it thrives—and then we keep that bed. The white form never succeeds here.

Rudbeckia. More dependable as an annual, fast-growing blackeyed susans nonetheless will often return for a second season and bloom two to three weeks before plugs planted a year after. It helps to leave quite a bit of stem and foliage, but not so much that disease develops—we try to cut back to about a foot high before winter comes. Plugs planted in the spring, slightly before the last frost date, can be manipulated toward a later bloom by cutting them back just before they bud, but make sure you leave enough foliage for regeneration. We've made the mistake of shearing to the ground and killed them.

Rudbeckias under shade grow taller with weaker stems, and the protection doesn't seem to alter their bloom time. We use Indian Summer for most of our sales, and Mexican Sunset for novelty buyers (we sell it as "Chocolate Susans"). We once grew green-centered Irish Eyes at a customer's request, but it had little market appeal. The double form of Rudbeckia sold poorly for us, and the true perennial Goldsturm, a spray-type, while popular, doesn't fit our irrigation methods since it's somewhat of a moisture hog, and so many other flowers come to bloom at the same time that it gets lost in the sales fray.

Scabiosa. The perennial Scabiosas may be the most valuable flower you can grow, as they continue to bloom all summer if you keep deadheading to prevent them from going to seed. We plant new crops using small plugs (200 trays) every spring. These will flower four or five weeks after those planted in earlier years start to bloom. After being cut for a month or more, older plants tend to throw increasingly weak stems and the cutters likely have given up deadheading properly. The first year plants then produce remarkably tall and rigid stems that exceed the quality of any cut earlier in the season. The new plantings, less prolific, continue to bloom past the frost, and if you cut back old plantings to just above the crowns (you need to leave most of the foliage or you may kill them) they too will bloom again with usable if less astonishing stems.

The perennial Scabiosa should be cut daily as it moves from bud to spent quite rapidly, with Ochroleuca, which sports a creamy, almost insignificant flower, going to unusable from bud in half a day (cut it before you see color, it will open). Knautia, almost indistinguishable in form from Scabiosa and grouped by root weevil into the same tasty column, should be treated the same when cutting as you can almost see it racing toward seedhood as you watch.

Veronica. Using different cultivars, you can stretch the Veronica season considerably, as about three weeks separate the earliest bloomers from the latest. You can also cut back Veronica before bloom since it will regrow and bloom later, or shear to the ground immediately after bloom for a second, late, but reliable harvest that will have somewhat shorter stems. Plant plugs at the beginning of the season for a bloom that comes shortly after those that have overwintered, though the stems may not be as impressive as those of older plants. Tall varieties may flop, but are usually prolific enough you won't mind losing a few stems. The white form Icicles sports a stronger stem and is on the shorter side, though grown in a shade house may reach three to four feet. It has a high mortality rate here so we only grow it on occasion.

Though an inexperienced flower grower might deem Veronica insignificant, its spiky form and color make it an important component for designs. It doesn't take up much space in the cooler and the van so, inch for inch, may be one of the most profitable species we grow.

Minor Demand Perennials

Species with minor demand give an added impression of large selection, so we plant a number of species that sometimes seem to be more trouble than they're worth but which we grow because customers call for them from time to time.

Aquilegia. Since Columbine comes early when few perennials are on, we'd love to have a good crop of it to sell. But the heat here often mutes its colors and the wind shreds its fragile petals, and aphids gravitate to it as if it were the latest ethnic restaurant. If we had a protected area or a large enough shade house, we would definitely grow this crop, especially the blue varieties. We grew the double form for a few years, but it shatters badly.

Brunnera. If you have a shady spot that's easy to care for (weed-free), you might try this crop for its earliness (May bloom) and true blue color. Easy to mistake for Forget-Me-Nots, it's not very prolific, somewhat insignificant in size and consequently a bit difficult to harvest—and might make you squeamish charging what it's worth—but commands interest when needed.

Campanula. The Cup and Saucers varieties of Campanula, while beautiful and long lasting, are difficult to design with, being somewhat coarse, and the Champion series that eliminates this coarseness has finicky needs that don't fit our climate even when we try it the greenhouse. Pyramidalis, another biennial like the Cup and Saucers, needs to be staked since it grows four and five feet tall, but its coarse look limits its appeal, too.

Persicifolia, a perennial that becomes less prolific after the first year of harvest (which comes after a winter of vernalization), makes the A list some years, its earliness, shape and colors perfect for June wedding work. Though it's easily overwatered, somewhat susceptible to rust, prone to short stems at times and lodging at others, we plant it every other year to have a constant supply. It sometimes flies off the truck in large amounts, and some years sells hardly at all.

Catmint (Nepeta). Catmint, not CatNIP, with which clients and often our competitors often confuse it. A lousy flower by my standards, still we sell quite a bit as it blooms early and has a nice clear blue, plus a fragrance that not just cats appreciate. Plant a short row, cut it back heavily after harvest, harvest in another month then cut and harvest and cut again. Later harvests seem prone to bee activity that inspires blooms to brown, but some clients buy Catmint even in bud to use as an interesting foliage. Though suppliers may sell some varieties as non-seeding, don't believe them—some just seed LESS, still too much.

Convallaria. Lily of the Valley would be an A list plant if it grew all season long. Very fragrant and universally loved as a bridal bouquet component, it commands a price as high as six dollars a stem out of season despite its small stature. Unfortunately, in season it can bloom prolifically but has a very small market. A clever grower can order pips almost all year long, plant them and have flowers in thirty days. We've never possessed the required abilities of planning to do such a thing, however, and we lack the large clientele needed to make it work. Needs shade to increase its height.

Dicentra. The good news: Bleeding Hearts bloom early in the spring when little else does. The bad news: the Bleeding Heart bloom doesn't tolerate hard frost. Since we suffer frequent harsh cold spells in the spring, rather than the milder temperature swings of most climates, our crop fails more frequently than it succeeds—so we've abandoned it. Dicentra falls into the rare category of perennials that perform quickly in the greenhouse, though, so a crop planted in the fall produces well early the next spring—too early for our market, but those with a wider market windows might benefit from this species. Designers sometimes find Bleeding Hearts difficult to work with, since their sprawling form requires a bit more cleverness for incorporation.

Echinacea. Though Echinacea comes in so many colors and fragrances now that you'd think it an essential cut flower, we struck it from our list because of its bulkiness at a time when many other species come to bloom. We just don't have room for it. Grasshoppers appreciate this flower in a way florists don't. Some of the varieties closer to the parent species have droopy petals that buyers interpret as wilting and therefore avoid.

Echinops. Globe Thistle's spherical, true blue head give it likeability on two fronts, and its long, stiff stem and excellent vase life only add to its charm (can a thistle have charm?). We've not discovered a way to lengthen its blooming season, but clients regularly ask for it out of season so it no doubt has a continuing market. Rust afflicts our crop every year, usually just shortly after bloom begins, making it a race between harvest and disease that we sometimes lose. Painted Lady caterpillars afflict Echinops just as they do all other thistles, and tend to move in as heads begin to form—watch carefully and spray or you'll lose the crop.

Eucomis. The Pineapple Lily needs to be heavily mulched in zone 5 but it will survive. What designers do with its tropical look I don't know but they do buy all of the stems we grow (only 200 or so).

Filipendula. This species, which has excellent appeal to designers, would be on the A list if it had a longer bloom period, but it does keep well in the cooler so provides a longer sales time than many specialty cuts. We've tried Ulmaria, a white form that blooms later with a larger flower than the earlier and smaller Vulgaris (our go-to variety), and which can be used as a raspberry like foliage—its bloom tends to look dull or dirty so lacks the appeal of the airier meadowsweets. We've tried Venusta, a tall pink variety, but it comes when the perennial glut strikes so we dropped it from our list. After many years of losing part of the Filipendula crop to wind and rain, which makes for tangled and twisted stems, we now apply netting the second it bolts to keep the crop upright.

Cut Filipendula Vulgaris the second the tiny center bloom swells and let it open in the cooler. You can wait until it opens to harvest but it doesn't take long to go from perfect to shattering. On high temperature days you may want to cut twice to stay ahead of the bed.

Gaura. Gaura's grasslike foliage sports white blossoms similar in shape to but smaller than Acidanthera's. They bloom from bottom to top of the spike, also like Acidanthera. Unfortunately, each blossom doesn't last long, but cut in bud it continues to bloom along the stem so works well for events.

Hellebores. We were really excited about Hellebores, since they bloom early when little else is available and have a look that appeals to the high-end flower connoisseur. Unfortunately, though our two hundred foot row of Hellebores seems to be thriving, after three years we've harvested almost nothing. The Hellebore bloom needs to be well developed in order to last well in the vase, and our quick and severe frosts almost always damage a crop before it's ready. Hence, our climate says "no" though our clients say "yes". In an area of milder climate fluctuations, Hellebores might be a real winner for March and April sales.

Heuchera. This species' tiny blooms might lead you to think it an unmarketable flower, but the variety "Firefly" sports such a striking coral that clients willingly pay eighty cents a stem (making a one gallon bucket worth well over a hundred dollars). No doubt other varieties with an equal appeal exist, and some clients ask for the foliage but our climate doesn't inspire the kind of attractive growth they're looking for.

Knautia. With a bloom identical in shape to but smaller than Scabiosa's, Knautia finds favor with some designers primarily for its deep burgundy color. One of the earliest perennials to bloom, it's also quick to seed, requiring cutting daily. Easily overwatered, Knautia acts much like delphinium, stubbornly clinging to life for several years when it's happy where it is, giving up after a season or two if placed where it's not.

Kniphofia. Some designers love the vivid colors of Red Hot Pokers, but only one variety makes it through our winters on even a semi-consistent basis. Flamenco throws enough stems even the first year to pay for planting plugs, but since it grows short due to our high intensity light it moves on and off our list of offerings. We tried it under shade to inspire height but failed to get much bloom.

Lavender. After several attempts, we've abandoned this crop, which marginally survives in our climate. We tried Munstead, Grosso, Fred Boutin, Betty's Blues, and Graves, finding Betty's Blues the tallest and best color and most prolific, and though we planted different varieties to stretch the season of bloom only a few days separated the earliest from latest (our climate tends to compress the seasons for all plants). We get a fairly wide call for lavender bunches, sometimes in very large amounts, but because lavender can be a difficult cut and because we often lose the crop to bees, whose pollinating affects the blooms adversely by turning them brown before we can cut them, we're abandoning our plot.

Don't cut lavender back too severely, especially in the fall, or it won't recover. Instead, just shear it above the crown in late spring.

Lamb's Ears. While species Lamb's Ears sells fine, Stachys Helen Von Stein has a much bigger leaf and is less likely to go to seed. A few bunches of these go on the truck each week when we have room, but it's not such a big seller that we go overboard and sometimes we don't cut it at all if we have plenty of other product. Grasshoppers love it so it must be sprayed weekly and it's not an easy cut. We use Felcos and just cut field bunches that include mostly leaves, as this variety throws fewer stems with flowers.

Lobelia. Only the Fan series Lobelia has worked for us, but it must be grown under shade or it grows too short to harvest. Though a perennial, it needs no vernalization (as some Lobelias do) and performs as an annual here. The blue Fan especially turns designers' eye, but the perennial blue species form, Siphilitica, did not work for us, being quite coarse in look.

Lupine. No flower proves as fickle as lupine, which might shed its petals as it stands in the field or, unfortunately, as you hand it to a client. Then again, it might last ten to fourteen days in the vase—you just never know. Russell Lupines, the blue "The Governor" and the red "The Pages", may be the most astonishing of all flowers, stunning in a vase by themselves and just jaw-dropping in the field, qualities which surpass their drawbacks, though another attribute, its need for the acidic soil we lack, makes it difficult to grow in our area—and still every couple years I try it again. Our only luck has come on our first farm, where the gravelly soil, despite being alkaline, provided enough drainage for lupine to thrive. Once in a while woolly aphids may infest it.

Oregano. We grew Herrenhausen Oregano for years with moderate success in sales, but when we found Hopley's Purple we knew we had a winner. Herrenhausen has a short harvest window, needing to be cut before the pink flowers appear, while Hopley's looks good for weeks as it continues to form blooms which leave attractive pods behind them, and it has a much more usable form. A bed will produce for years and years.

Penstemon. Strictus, easy to grow and prolific, presents a vivid blue hard to find in the flower world, but like all Penstemons it sheds its lower blooms as the upper ones open, limiting its desirability. Still, it has its place, particularly in that wild, country (weedy, in some circles) look. Likewise, Jingle Bells, a taller, coral Penstemon, finds favor when designers call for that specific color. We tried Husker Red, but our soil gives it that alkaline look that just shouts "more iron". An early blooming aphid favorite.

Sedum. The tall Sedums, from the most common Autumn Joy that most people are familiar with, to Mohrchen, a dark leaved cultivar, command florist attention with both foliage and flower and have a long cutting period. Aphids tend to gravitate to Sedum before almost any other plant, and controlling them proves difficult because any moisture left on the leaves by spraying magnifies sunlight that damages the foliage. Sometimes we abandon this crop for just that reason, but sometimes the early aphid problem goes away by late summer and we then harvest.

Thalictrum. Having foliage much like Columbine and blossoming at a similar time, Thalictrum Delayavi's lavender blooms seem somewhat insignificant and easily shed. Cut this plant early in bloom or even earlier for foliage. Thalictrum Rochebrunianum, a much larger variety with a much bigger, yellow flower head needs staking as it can hit six feet tall.

Thermopsis. The earliest perennial to bloom, sometimes in mid-April, Thermopsis looks exactly like lupine but bears an electric yellow no lupine cultivar has. Its earliness often results in damage by hard frosts, but trim it back and it grows again, blooming prolifically. Bumblebees love Thermopsis, so you may need to cut it earlier than you like, before the flowers senesce.

ANNUALS

Annuals frequently sport a long cutting season and tend to bloom later in the year, filling out the availability list as the number of available perennials shrinks. These are some we grow (and some we don't).

Calendula. This is another aphid favorite, so we only grow it when we've forgotten the difficulty of controlling the pesky insects. It grows short here, often unusably so, and the central stem, which blooms first, can be so massive that three of four bunches will fill a bucket.

Not our favorite, but customers love the color.

Cerinthe. A quick grower, Cerinthe comes in handy when you need something to fill in a space in the greenhouse when the plug producer shorts you. Inside a house it grows taller and weaker, while outside it tends to be shorter and bushier. While a striking plant by itself, it loses its focal interest when put in arrangements so works best as a filler foliage. Its striking blue blooms get lost, but the blue-green leaves are unrivalled in the plant world as we know it. On a bad aphid year, Cerinthe is an obvious target.

Cosmos. Many, many years ago we grew Cosmos Sensation Mix and tried to sell it as a mix but had no luck at all. We refrained from growing it again until our best client asked us to, then marketed it in separate colors and found we could sell scads (though we do omit pink singles from the list). Designers like both the cranberry red and the white Cosmos, especially Double Click. Cutting cosmos is a challenge in the wind, so take Dramamine before doing so, and keep your cosmos bed deadheaded or it can easily get out of hand. Cut single forms in the bud, when barely cracked, and let them open in the cooler. Any not cut on the proper day will be spent the next, as the window for cutting is very short. Wait longer, if you wish, when cutting double varieties—they're more forgiving.

You can stagger a second crop of cosmos by seeding a crop a month later than the first. When the first bed escapes your control, the second plot comes in handy.

Daucus. Sometimes called Black Carrot, more often wrongly called Ammi, Daucus looks like Queen Anne's Lace but provides a wider color range that includes white, pink, shades of bronze-y red and black. It direct seeds well, lasts in the vase, and has strong appeal. This will be a staple for years to come.

Foxglove. Neither a desert crop nor a crop for alkaline soil—nonetheless we grow it. Outside we plant plugs just before the last frost date for mid summer harvest, but our stems sometimes stretch only to just over a foot, making them almost a different species compared to the same plants grown in the greenhouse. There, four foot, elegant spikes soar so magnificently toward the ceiling that you may feel it a crime to cut them were a check not waiting for their delivery. Planted in the greenhouse in February as plugs, they flower in May and June, but we plant in August to give them the added oomph that provides better, taller and earlier spikes in the spring. We plant only Camelot series but others may work well, too. They do not overwinter outside for us, and even in the hoophouse will die if they do not sufficiently root before hard winter hits. Without fail, spider mites show up on the indoor crop so check frequently and early, because when their presence becomes obvious it's too late to affect their populations.

Lisianthus. This species hits the B list for its high cost and its susceptibility to fungus both at the root and on the bloom, but makes the A list for its market appeal. Amateur flower shoppers sometimes mistake Lisianthus for a rose since it has a similar shape (though more delicate petals), so you can imagine how desirable designers find it. Growers in warmer climates have a much longer market window for this crop than growers in cold areas, as even varieties bred to bloom a month or more apart compress harvest into a couple weeks here. Applying shade slows a crop considerably, but late Lisianthus here becomes subject to humid nights that instigate botrytis in the bloom, destroying the crop.

Lisianthus plugs often cost double what most annual flowers do, and in areas closer to airport hubs the competition drives market prices down to where growing it may be unprofitable. Here, we charge a dollar a stem and customers gladly pay it (though other suppliers charge half that), because most have never seen Lisianthus outside of a box, where it's unusually prone to disease and wilt and rarely ships well or lasts. We often have to convince designers of its longevity, since anything they've purchased from a box performed poorly.

Lisianthus grows best in the coddling situation a greenhouse provides, blooming earlier and growing taller than those grown outside. But because it takes a fairly long time to get from plug to bloom, I prefer not to spend extra time and effort babying it inside.

Matricaria. A staple for us. We only grow Vegmo single, which looks so much like Chamomile that almost all our clients order it as such (and we no longer argue). We sometimes grow the green center variety, but clients prefer the wild look and after several trials with other varieties (there are a lot of them) Vegmo single rose to the top. If we have room in the greenhouse, we plant an early flat in February, and maybe one in the hoophouse a few weeks later, but outside Matricaria, planted in mid to late April (it will survive a hard frost, even as a plug), blooms only a week or two later than that babied inside for weeks if not months, so we mostly forego inside planting and instead concentrate on successive crops outside. Matricaria, though grown best as an annual, usually makes it through even harsh winters here, and this second-year crop provides the first cut that the earliest planted plugs of spring soon follow. Subsequent plantings (they need to be spread out by at least three to four weeks) make for continuous harvest. Cut the crops back severely immediately after harvest for a second flush. Matricaria can be weedy if you let it seed, so don't hang on to a crop too long or you'll have it in the strangest places.

Cut as field bunches, Matricaria harvests rapidly since it blooms somewhat evenly and has a wide window of cutting—from petals just showing to fully blown, but not seeded.

Papaver. Icelandic poppies need a long period of cool weather, which we provide with shade. We plant Champagne series plugs in mid-April (they survive hard frosts well) and begin harvest by mid-June. Planted in a heated house in February they bloom in May but finish in mid-June, due to high heat. Susceptible to fungal diseases in humid conditions, sometimes a few die during wet weather periods.

Poppies hold best if cut just as the pod cracks, for if left to open on their own their very fragile petals get beaten by wind, lose their color to sun, develop transparencies in just a couple hours, and draw bees so voraciously that pollen forms almost immediately. Almost all stems of a variety bloom at the same time in the morning, for a brief hour or two, so watch them closely and then rest for the remainder of the day.

A prolific flowerer, Icelandic Poppies last well in the vase, unlike Orientals, but you may have to convince designers who have only seen them shipped in boxes, where tight quarters and a long out-of-water period hastens their senescence.

Queen Anne's Lace. While more gentle climates allow growers to direct seed Ammi Majus, here the springs are short and hot weather forces it to bolt, so plugs provide the only way to get a suitable cut flower stem. Since it will handle hard frosts we plant it in mid-April, nearly a month before the last frost date, and harvest it around the Fourth of July, when white is popular. A couple weeks after Ammi harvest, its sister variety Green Mist comes to bloom, with a tighter bloom and a better vase life, as well as a longer harvest window and blooming more prolifically. Rarely afflicted by pests, on a bad aphid year it can still become a target.

Scabiosa. We plant annual varieties as plugs a week before the last frost date, and they're such prolific producers that we shear half of the 200 back to crown level approximately a week before we expect them to bud. This delays their bloom to a date that closely follows the last cuts of the unpruned crop. These later blooms will be shorter but that's a good thing, as the earlier Scabiosa, which can become quite tall, often lodges if the weather includes both wind and rain. We sell Ace of Spades, Black Knight, and the red varieties but forego white and blue, two redundant colors that just compete with the perennial Scabiosas already in bloom.

Snapdragons. Oh, snaps, where to start. Breeders have stretched the snap season so that they can be harvested all year, so you'll have to experiment your entire career to get the varieties and techniques down that serve you best. They've split them into 4 groups, those in 1 growing in cool, winter situations, with proper environments warming as you move from 2 to 3 to 4, the latter two more appropriate for late, outdoor crops. We start with plugs from the 2 group in the heated house the first week in February for a mid May to mid June harvest, but if you have more money for heat than we do or live in a warmer zone you can certainly plant sooner. Chantilly snaps bloom earliest and can either be planted twice as thickly as regular snaps (two to a six inch netting square) or pinched for multiple blooms that come a little later. If cut back after harvest they will bloom again with varying degrees of success—it may be too hot in a greenhouse situation to bring a second flush of harvestable blooms, and even outdoors severe heat can ruin a second harvest—though if you time it right, a very late harvest when cool weather returns in the fall becomes possible.

Outside, snaps planted early (we sometimes plant a full three weeks before the last frost date) will survive considerable cold, particularly if hardened off, and even when frozen by a sudden cold snap often come back from their deadened stalks, but with more stems. Snaps that are cut down before bloom will come back if you wish a later harvest, and harvested stems can be severely cut back for a second flush about a month or six weeks later. When cutting back, remember that the deeper the cut, the longer the second flush of stems will be (this is often, though not always, true for most species of flowers and shrubs).

Because snaps flop easily, we've taken to netting them even in the field, though the support required outside is minimal compared to that needed indoors. Expect as many as ten stems a plant on Rocket snaps per cutting.

Aphids tend to enjoy the succulent stems and foliage, so be on the lookout—an early remedy really beats dealing with an aphid explosion.

Sunflowers. Most sunflowers open even if cut when only a single petal has lifted from the head, but our customers often want them ready to use so we wait until the petals become perpendicular to the head or even later. Waiting to cut allows insects access and wind and sun to burn petals, so pick your poison, cut early or late, depending on your circumstances.

When planting sunflowers be aware of their blooms' tendency to move with the sun, so plant for easy access as it's simpler to cut when facing rather than when behind them (though you'll get so you can even do this). I often plant two sets of two rows (two tractor passes) side by side, to lessen the number of walk rows, but access is much easier if you plant half that—with two rows spaced eighteen inches apart, and a walk row on each side, you can cut either in the morning or evening and have the suns face you at either time.

Aphids will pressure sunflowers in the right conditions, so I often take a quick walk down rows that look three or four weeks from bloom, pull a leaf and examine the underside. Generally aphids work sunflowers from the ground up, so be especially aware of the oily, black honeydew that aphids exude on lower leaves—if the weeders have left a sowthistle, for instance, the aphids that started there will move to sunflowers nearby and their population will explode. Spot spray and be extra diligent for the remainder of the year, because likely the problem will continue. Occasionally, the aphid problem can become so bad that they infest a head before it even opens, destroying the crop.

As noted above, we use Vincents and succession plant.

Sweet Peas. In terms of dollars per square foot, sweet peas take the marketing crown. You could drive a Volkswagen Beetle filled with sweet peas on your route and make a living, since fifteen stems at eight dollars takes up almost no room. They don't ship well, giving the local grower an advantage, and if you live in a cold area like we do you can extend the availability late into the summer when they can't be grown in hot climates. And everyone likes sweet peas, even the farmer's market customer who'd never buy another flower.

Since we've never found a sweet pea plug producer we start our earliest peas in 72 size trays about the first of January, and they're ready to put in the greenhouse ground a month later. We use Sunshine Series peas exclusively now, after growing cheaper varieties for over a decade. Little did we know that plant breeders are sometimes honest with their pitches!

The Sunshines are so superior in size and growth habit that they're worth their considerable cost, and they have a wide color range. We set the plugs directly in the ground, six to twelve inches apart, in the center of the greenhouse and when they start to flop hang netting from the eight foot high center purlin. Since the netting comes in four foot increments we need two passes, one above the other, attached together with zip ties (thank you zip ties, thank you rebar, thank you duct tape). We space T-posts every 8-10 feet to keep them more secure. Sweet peas, being unruly, need somewhat constant attention, so once a week you may have to run string or twine on the outside of the netting to keep the rogue vines on their path toward the ceiling—or thread vines through the netting if you're so inclined. Sometime around May 1 these will bloom.

Meanwhile, we've germinated another set for the rollup house and planted them about April 1. They'll take a great deal of frost, surviving even down to the teens. These peas start blooming in early to mid June, about when the greenhouse peas start playing out because of heat. We also grow a third crop of peas by direct seeding in mid to late April for a July and August harvest. In the past, we've always grown these under shade, but last year we tried an experiment by planting a crop outside in a north–south row with a long season sunflower planted in the next row to the west to provide protection from the hot afternoon sun. The added morning light must be to the sweet peas' liking as they outperformed the shadehouse peas in size of bloom, color, and vigor.

The sweet peas that come in late July and August lose their quality as heat increases, but clients also get less picky since the locally grown peas are still better than those coming from hot areas. By early to mid-August the crop has played out. A fall crop might be possible but we shut down in mid-September so have never tested it.

A ninety foot row of sweet peas may yield three to five hundred usable stems a day. We sometimes cut them on two to three foot vines, rather than as stems, just to slow the plants down. We harvest vine peas in ten stem bunches, rather than the usual fifteen, and find they last better in the cooler and the vase than stem peas, which tend to deteriorate fairly rapidly under any conditions.

Zinnias. We grow Benary's Giants, or the cheaper knockoff variety that copies them, for their size and strong color selection. Zinnias grow quickly, blooming so prolifically that deadheading on a regular basis becomes essential. Because they last poorly in the vase and won't take cooler temperatures lower than 45 for very long, harvest must wait until the day before delivery. Since we only have two main delivery days, many blooms go unharvested and must be deadheaded, as zinnias tend to shut down as soon as seed formation begins. Despite the extra work, zinnias pull their weight on the farm, finding favor with progressive designers—though shunned by traditional florists for being old-fashioned.

Cut zinnias when fully open, but before pollen starts to show, as once cut they do not open further. The green variety tends to produce many oddly formed flowers so requires more deadheading and takes longer to cut—and also draws aphids sooner than the other colors.

Less Important Annuals

Amaranthus, despite its majestic beauty, lacks big market appeal. Primarily because of its sometimes immense size, it works into arrangements only with difficulty—it's more a hotel lobby flower than a dining room centerpiece. If you pinch this crop back severely it throws smaller, more usable stems, but the crop comes so fast and the market's so small that much of even a meager planting goes to waste. And since an Amaranth head contains about a million seeds (no exaggeration, that), leaving a single stalk in the field means weeding for years afterward. The gold form, Hot Biscuits, sells better than the Burgundy types like Opopeo.

Atriplex, known as Orach to vegetable growers, comes in a nice lime green and a burgundy. Designers here prefer the green. A seed head with thousand of flat discs, it can be mistaken as an immature hydrangea at a distance. Since it grows to eight feet high at times you might feel you need to stake it (we don't), and you do want to remove it from the field before it self-seeds for future unwanted harvests.

Clarkia Unguiculata, a wildflower that's hard to find but whose seed comes cheap, can be succession sowed from the moment the soil's workable to mid-July for continuous harvests. Its jewel-toned colors unrivaled by almost any other flower, it misses the A list for its fickleness in the vase—since its tip bends, perception tells the buyer it's wilting, though that is its natural state. It also sheds, its lower flowers falling as the buds above open, but as a spiky flower with vibrant colors it works well for events, and a clever and bold designer will be thrilled to see this on your truck.

The small seed, to be surface sown, requires continual moisture, so later crops may be more difficult to germinate.

Cleome. What a beautiful plant this is, with a large bloom but very prickly stem. Eight stems make a very big bunch of good value, but the petals shed and thus make it somewhat undesirable. Still, it's a stunning flower and if you have room in the field and the cooler, try it.

Godetia, a close relative of Clarkia but much better known, though stunning and inviting with its bold colors, sometimes misses our planting list completely, mainly because it comes when product from other species abounds. Its shortness presents a problem, too, since at fourteen inches it just barely rises above the lip of a short Procona. It can be a difficult cut since, if harvested in bud, designers can't see its true worth, and if harvested later the fragile petals often suffer damage. Grown under shade, we find it too lanky and weak as it gains two feet in height. A single plant easily produces ten to twenty stems.

If you've seen Lavatera (Rose Mallow, another annual of marginal interest) or even Hollyhocks, you already know the form of this flower's bloom. Salpiglossis also has a similar look, but has very fragile petals that defy the most careful harvester.

Helichrysum, strawflowers, makes our list on alternate years. Its weak stem makes it a poor cut flower, but its strong colors make it desirable—and the fact we can fit a lot in a bucket makes it pleasing to us.

Larkspur tricks us every year; we never know how to appraise it. Often, it blooms at the same time as our Delphinium, the form of which is nearly identical but more appealing and larger. But if the bloom times don't coincide the market for larkspur greatly expands, and since it blooms during wedding season we plant mostly white. Larkspur always comes when harvest from other flowers is heavy, so because it blooms very fast it often gets away from us. Inevitably, as soon as we make the last successful cut, designers start asking for more. Someday we'll discover the proper timing and extend the season properly.

If you plant larkspur in the fall, make sure to do so in a well–drained area—soggy soil drowns it. If it survives the winter, it blooms two to three weeks earlier than that planted in early spring, growing much taller and sturdier, as well.

Nigella, love-in-a-mist, can hardly be rivaled in form, texture and color. Cut in tight bud, both the blue and white Miss Jekyll will open in the cooler, but both sell better if customers see their open blooms, so we cut them as field bunches with some fully open, some in the bud—this seems to strike the right chord for marketing to our clientele. We never sell all we plant so leave a few to go to pod, but these will reseed if left in the field.

Salvia Victoria Blue performs the same design function as Veronica, but tends to be difficult for many designers to hydrate. Victoria White has very strong color but browns easily, so might do better in a greenhouse where bees can't get to it. Perennial Salvias come earlier than most perennials, giving an early start to the season, but their appeal dwindles when Veronica, which has similar form, shape and color, appears on the van.

Stock, or Matthiola, must be raised in the greenhouse here, since early summer heat sends it to bloom when it's very short. Under plastic it needs to be planted by early March for a May and June bloom, spaced closely at two plugs to the net square. Plantsmen have bred enough varieties to lengthen the bloom period out considerably, to such length that those bred to be late sometimes don't flower for us, instead aborting.

Talinum has been named "nerdberry" by a client for its likeness to the candy. Its tiny red berries give airiness to a design but its use is limited. Easy to cut, though, either as a field bunch or stem by stem.

Verbena Bonariensis, though a poor cut flower in my mind, grows prolifically and tall and despite shedding badly continues to be a designer favorite. Its small, purple-lavender bloom comes on a square stem that is sturdy and long, and bunched as either a field bunch, which is much easier to cut, or as a twelve or fifteen stem bunch, it doesn't take up much room on a truck but brings considerable income. Through clever pruning either before bloom or after, harvesting continuously becomes possible.

Other annuals sometimes listed as cuts but which don't work for us include Agrostemma (subject to rust, difficult to cut, small bloom) and Tweedia (hard to hydrate).

BULBS

Warmer climates provide a proper environment for many more bulb species than we can grow even with the aid of greenhouses. The species listed below work for our climate and short marketing season.

Allium. Because Idaho exports so much onion seed and grows most of the onions used for U.S. food consumption, it's illegal to import Allium flower bulbs (an onion is an Allium) to Idaho, due to disease threat, so our experience is limited. Easy to grow here and difficult to kill, we have a twelve year old bed we've not irrigated for ten years and which we've sprayed glyphosate on a number of times. We also have an eight year old bed intended to replace the earlier one which refuses to die, and a five year old bed that seems to be thriving, as well. Purple Sensation, because of its mid-range softball size, works best for us, though the much later and much smaller Drumstick Allium performs and sells well—but it comes at a time when we have plenty of other product. The very large, early Alliums command double the price but sell in smaller amounts. They also seem to lose their vigor more rapidly; Christophii has a basketball size bloom on a one foot stem that has some appeal, the bright yellow but short Moly is well received, and if you want to stink up the truck and wow your customers with an unusual Allium relative, plant Nectaroscordum—you'll sell a lot the first week when customers see the alien, Dr. Seussy shape, then not a stem the next after they've caught a whiff. Think "skunk". We put a bit of bleach in the water of Allium buckets to alleviate some of the oniony smell that the stems emit.

Brodiae, a small, weedy bulb, is hardy only to zone 6 so when we grow it we plant in crates in either the hoophouse or the greenhouse to afford it protection. It's an easy cut with the look of a miniature Agapanthus, its blue a favorite with designers and its open, Allium like head a space-taker that gives both airiness and fullness to a work.

Hyacinths. Hyacinths can be grown much like tulips, in trenches, in crates, in multiple seasons in the greenhouse, hoophouse, and outside, but are much more susceptible to erratic frosts so we no longer grow them. Unprotected, a crop succumbs to frosts when in bud.

Pull hyacinths, bulbs and all, for sale to give extra height. Many florists like to have the bulb so they can plant it in their own gardens. This means the soil you plant them in must be porous and soft, or you will break the stem as you pull or dig. You then need to wash the soil off, adding to the difficulty.

Lilies. We don't work with lilies much, as our clients shy away from traditional flowers, but we have, over the years, dipped into the market when a whim arises, growing both Asiatic and Orientals in crates in the houses and outside. Because of our erratic weather and frequent severe late frosts, we found that only first year lilies provide a reliable crop outside. Unlike a lot of plants, lilies won't take any frost and perform afterwards, so those we harvested the first year may freeze three or four springs in a row before we get another harvest.

Lilies have an advantage over many crops as bulb suppliers can keep them dormant and sell them to you as you need them, and with charts detailing the days it takes for a given cultivar to bloom it's fairly simple to grow and harvest one crop after another by planting successively. You will need to make adjustments in your scheduling, since a ten day window between plantings in February or April will result in a different harvest window than the same ten days in the hotter months of June or July, and the chart numbers created for perfect temperatures will change, too, the season lengthening if you grow at colder temperatures and shortening with more heat. You'll also need to adjust what size bulbs you buy by your clients' likes—some feel a lot of buds are just in the way, allowing you to buy cheaper, smaller bulbs. And then there's the numbers adjustments needed, as most suppliers like to sell in crate-size increments that might vary from 250 to 400, when you may only need 50 or a 100 for your small market.

The omnipresence of lilies at the bulb supply level means omnipresence in the flower supply chain, unfortunately. Because lilies are used in a widespread market in large amounts, they flow through the flower chain from every source, making competition fierce. But a local grower willing to push into the market and persevere (there'll be resistance—many florists have had standing lily orders for years with their regular wholesaler, so they'll not be open to change), all the while maintaining quality, will eventually acquire a dependable clientele. It takes great organizational abilities, though, to keep a supply of a product constant without creating an oversupply, as lilies come on fast and tend not to hold as long or as well as other flowers in the cooler. Once you've ironed out the slack in production and harvest to make it manageable, and once you've ironed out the slack in the sales chain so you have a constant demand, you may find lilies to be a more dependable product than many of the other species you grow.

Muscari, commonly called grape hyacinths, can be grown like tulips, using the three season method. Because they multiply very rapidly and may be difficult to dig up, plant them in crates, then bury the crates, and retrieve them as necessary when you want to replant them somewhere else, or throw them away.

Narcissus. Daffodils clog the flower supply chain for much of late winter and spring, coming to designers at very low prices impossible for small growers to meet. Luckily, so many varieties of Daffodils exist that unusual types evade the big producers' purview. Any fragrant type, no matter how short, grabs designers' imaginations, as does any unusually colored double. We try to plant three or four new types each year in the hoophouse, then move these out to the field for second, third, and fourth year harvests. They don't command the French Tulip price, but they're easy to cut and come at a time when you have little else to sell. A hard frost may abort the flowers, which should normally be harvested as the bloom begins to nod, but is not yet open.

Ranunculus and Anemones. We treat these short day bloomers alike since their habits are almost identical: similar bloom time, similar growth temperature needs, similar susceptibilities to diseases. In zone 5 these two crops (throw in Freesia for another like species) are tricky, as they don't like frost but will survive mild ones, preferring cool temperatures to both cold and hot. It's too expensive to heat a house through long periods of below zero weather without a guaranteed market to sell them, so we've tried these crops many ways (all inside):

1) Early plant in September, heating to just above freezing in winter. This is the perfect way to

grow them, but our heater blew out on a fifteen degree below zero windy night, giving the crop a spell of about eight hours at fifteen above. This damaged the full grown plants severely, so we sheared back the melted foliage. The crop recovered for a March and April harvest of 8000 stems in a 20 x 48 house. Unfortunately, at that time of year our clients need far fewer than that so we composted two thirds of the stems.

2) Plant in October, hoping for less foliage growth, placing a curtain to shorten the area in the house to be heated. This works better, but opening and closing the curtain each day is annoying (the curtain needs to be opened to allow fans to move humid air out during the day).

3) Plant in very early spring (February) using plugs. We harvested only two stems a plant, barely paying for the plugs and expenses.

4) Plant in early November, so plants just barely emerge and can easily be covered at nights, with warmer ground temperatures competing favorably with dropping air temperatures. We cover with a double layer construction plastic that has an air layer, rather than Remay. Though more expensive, it lasts longer and provides more protection. The close-to-the-ground ranunculus take temperatures as low as 10, so we only cover when outside temperatures are expected to fall below that level. These

ranunculus,, having less foliage, survive disease-free but still bloom in mid-March.

We've also tried hydronic, root zone heating, hoping a warmer ground might make up for cold air temperatures (it doesn't win that battle). In all cases, both anemones and ranunculus shut down in mid May, possibly from long light periods, possibly from the higher heat than can't be controlled in the covered houses. One might be able to pull the plastic from a house where these crops are started early and lengthen the season, but we find putting plastic on and off to be the least pleasant job on the farm so have never tried that method.

Ranunculus and anemones provide an extra product to sell with tulips, but their small size and short stature don't command the interest that French tulips do.

Tulips. In a harsh, desert climate tulips often fare poorly, being battered by high, hot winds and washed out by constant sunlight, not to mention suffering sporadic hard frosts that turn foliage black in the morning and leave stems lying flat on the ground, only to, in the best of circumstances, green up and stand by late afternoon, though perhaps with a twist to remember weather by. Nonetheless, we do grow tulips outside here, but grow them in a greenhouse and a hoophouse too, giving us three crops of a harvest than spans 10-12 weeks. All the bulbs go in the ground in October so they get the necessary cold period before emerging in the spring, but the ten thousand in the greenhouse emerge about February 1 and with the aid of heat to keep temperatures slightly above freezing at night, start blooming six weeks later.

The ten thousand in a roll up hoophouse emerge slightly later but, being without heat, take longer to come to bloom, harvest starting almost immediately when the last flowers get cut in the greenhouse. To get a four week harvest from a crop, plant cultivars (we use mostly French tulips—another word for "big", parrots or doubles, though we sometimes throw in a viridiflora or something appealing enough to make up for smaller blooms) that flower early, like World's Favorite or the Impression series, then stagger later blooming varieties and ending up with Maureen, Avignon, Dordogne, Grand Style or others, which bloom almost a month later. Then, in the second house, plant a like schedule, with the early tulips coming on as the late ones in the first house finish, repeating the variety sequence.

Since outdoor temperatures rise, the harvest in the hoophouse shrinks to three weeks here, after which the outdoor tulips repeat the process, their bloom starting just as the hoophouse finishes. We plant less outside for a couple reasons. First, a greater loss results from aberrant weather patterns (heads can be frozen by very cold temperatures, can be blistered by hot winds, can be twisted from falling down on cold nights and rising again, and be eaten or lain upon by deer). Secondly, the outdoor crop, facing higher temperatures, squeezes the harvest period into an even tighter time span of only two weeks. The last tulips, while often of lesser quality, find a higher demand, since supply elsewhere diminishes. By late May tulips become difficult to bring in from other areas so ours are often the last to be sold, sometimes lasting into Memorial Day with the aid of a couple weeks in the cooler.

Tulips can be subject to fungal problems, so we rotate the beds each year, planting a middle bed and a side bed each year, then the other side and the other middle the next. This is an insufficient soil resting period for tulips, which we discover every time we get a long, wet period normally rare in this desert clime. Ten days of 95% humidity inspire a number of diseases to appear, and on occasion we've lost a third of our crop to "Tulip Fire", named aptly for its rapid sweep through a crop as it makes it unmarketable.

Non-flower growers are often astonished when they hear we plant twenty five thousand tulips, imagining us planting one at a time, trowel in hand. Often they ask why we don't have a machine (if you're the type of person who asks this, you might refrain from farming as you're likely prone to overcapitalization) to do the job, and I just tell them Jeriann can plant over a thousand an hour—and my speed isn't that far behind hers.

We just dig a three foot wide trench, four to six inches deep, pour a little sterile potting soil in the bottom of the pit to ward off a bit of the hidden fungal problem, then plant twelve to fifteen bulbs in a row, a finger's width between them. Five to six thousand bulbs fit in such a trench of a 96 x 20 foot house, leaving a

5 foot walkway on each end. We then cover the bulbs with potting soil, hand water in (if you buy bulk soil you may find this difficult, as dry peat will actually ride on water rather than absorb it, so make sure you check your watering so not just the surface is wet), lay three or four drip tape lines down the bed over the bulbs, then cover the drip tape with the dirt taken out of the trench. It's best to have the drip lines filled with water and operating, not just to check for breaks in the lines but to keep the lines in place as soil is thrown over them. By having the drip lines in the ground you avoid an annoying problem that occurs when they're left aboveground—the lines will ride up on the tulip foliage as it grows, consequently wetting the foliage and giving habitat for those pesky diseases.

French tulips, possibly due to their greater size which increase shipping costs and damage, somehow evade the efforts of big wholesalers, who push small tulips through the grocery store chains almost all winter and spring. This makes them an easy sale for the local grower who chooses to finagle a way into the supermarket. The cost of French tulip bulbs is sometimes no greater than that of smaller (but usually earlier blooming) tulips, but the French type command a much greater sales price.

Other bulbs we've grown include Ornithogalums (designers find all Ornithogalums appealing, but they bloom before our markets are fully developed) and Crocosmia (another designer favorite, but marginally hardy here and prone to rust, thrips and spider mites).

UGLIES AND FOLIAGE

A client of ours described her method of design as requiring a "pretty", some filler, and an "ugly". We don't use that last term (by which she meant texture) when marketing varieties, but a number of plants we grow qualify for her category. Rudbeckia Green Wizard keeps the center cone of a Blackeyed Susan, albeit a lengthened and enlarged one, while losing much of the petals' size and turning them green. Prone to powdery mildew, ours never make it to the later cutting stage that follows pollen shed, so we cut early, before the shed, selling all our crop and leaving clients asking for more. We plant a new crop every three years since it tends to die out over time. It won't bloom much the first year for us, though it might in warmer climates.

Nigellas usable as uglies include Stellata, Transformer, and the pods of love-in-a-mist. Albion Green may not look as much like a nice ugly as its deep burgundy brother, Albion Black, but cutting off the pod tops reveals an incredibly interesting, fruity look. Stellata, a Buckminster Fuller-like plant that looks like a cross between a geodesic dome and a ping pong ball, needs to be cut early before it shatters but after it blooms, a fairly short window, and Transformer, which looks like a coronet or the Burger King crown, often succumbs to rust so we no longer grow it. When successfully grown, however, it's well received.

Poppy pods of almost any sort find favor among designers, last well in the cooler and vase, and even dry well, holding their shape. The opium poppy, Somniferum, may be the most attractive of all, but you may be risking a police sting when you sell them, as it's technically illegal to grow. The Oriental poppies generate a nice pod, too. Just remember that any plant cut as a pod is nearing seed stage, so be sure you cut all the stems in the field and remove them if you don't want them to seed out and grow in following years.

Allium left to seed makes a nice ugly, too, though if bees don't adequately pollinate the flowers the resulting ball won't be marketable. Make sure you deadhead any Allium left beyond flower or you'll have a weedy crop to contend with for all time.

Bells of Ireland are another essential foliage for us, almost a signature plant for our business. We sometimes plant plugs in late winter in the greenhouse, but a fungus specific to Bells, cercospora, often afflicts the seed that plug producers use. Blotching the leaves with brown circles, it moves fast through a crop and though it's easily controlled with constant spraying we prefer "easy", so more often than not we wait until spring for planting.

Bell plugs take considerable cold, so are among our earliest outside plantings some three to four weeks before the last frost date. It's best to harden off, though we don't—instead, I watch the weather forecast to make sure three or four days will pass without below freezing nights. A second set of plugs go in around the last frost date, when we also direct seed a crop whose harvest will follow that of the plugs. Three weeks to a month later we will seed another crop, and again after that, and again as late as mid-July for September harvest. We thus have a continual harvest. Bells have a long harvest window, unlike most crops, stretching from the moment you think they look ready until they become papery and spiny a month later, and even harvested in the heat of the afternoon will recover from fully wilted to stiff and erect after a few hours in the cooler.

Dill has its adherents, so we plant it first thing in the spring, well before the last frost date, then plant a second crop a month later and another, and another. You want to adjust how much you plant to your market, because you definitely don't want to let dill go to seed or you'll be seeing it just about everywhere on your acreage. Cut after pollen shed but before it makes seed. Take any mature heads out of the field or send to an enemy.

Dill's foremost lover is the aphid. When scouting a field for the critters, I always check the dill crop since they show up there well before they do elsewhere. Look near ground level for their first appearance and take care of the problem early.

Grasses make good uglies. What makes grasses easy makes them difficult, however. Generally, they germinate well, making for a crop simple to grow, and generally, being easy to grow, they can become weedy—don't let them go to seed! We grow a number of grasses, starting with the early season (May) bloomer Melica and finishing with Miscanthus, Ravennae grass and Sorghastrum, which often bloom after we've put the route to bed. Chasmanthium, a perennial August bloomer, is generally our last grass for sales, though if I've seeded late crops of millet we have that, as well.

Foxtail Millet (looks like a lime green foxtail), Highlander Millet (more the shape of a cattail), Red Millet (a smaller head than foxtail, more erect, with a bronzy tinge) make up a large portion of our seeded crop, and we start with planting the first week of May (Foxtail and Red), then plant a different variety a week to ten days later (Highlander, which has a higher germination temperature). A mid-July or even early August planting will yield September harvests. Make sure you cut all these down before they start seeding, and you may have to remove the entire crop from the field—the heads will continue to complete seed formation even when you plow them under.

We also plant plugs of Briza Maxima, an annual quaking grass. For years we planted the perennial, Briza Media, but found it only really produced well after vernalization, a year later, and on subsequent years performed more and more poorly, though it's taller habit made it a better cut than Maxima.

Another grass, Frosted Explosion, is a terrible thing to let loose in the field, so be careful with this one, too. On our first acreage this species grew everywhere and I fought it constantly, only learning some years later that designers were actually using it and PAYING FOR IT. It took Jeriann a couple years to convince me to grow it, but now it's a staple and I seed a second crop about a month after the first, but always make sure every stem has been taken out of the field, burned or bagged.

Occasionally, aphids afflict Frosted Explosion and the millets, in our experience on the years that aphids bother nothing else (go figure).

The most remarkable of herbs for the florist trade but little used, Sage Berggarden is a round-leafed variety that does not flower, and though supposedly hardy to only zone 6 has come back for twelve years now on our zone 5 farm. It looks pretty ratty in the spring, so needs to be cut back severely—but not too severely, or you can kill it: like lavender, it needs some buds on the stem to rejuvenate. Grown outside, it tends to be quite short in this high-light desert, but 8-10 inches seems tall enough for our customers. Some years we get a second crop from the same plot. Grown under shade, it picks up another 4-8 inches in height, and planted in a rollup house in April it will provide for two cuttings in the same year—three in warmer zones, no doubt. We net it when planting it under cover. Grown in a greenhouse, even without heat, it will take zero degree temperatures and still look marketable. Each plant should provide about half a field bunch per cutting the first year, while on subsequent years the harvest increases.

Sage Officinalis, the common garden sage, requires a bit more cleverness since it flowers with a form and color that few designers appreciate. If cut back a couple weeks before it's expected to bloom it will continue to grow without trying to re-flower, putting its energy instead into the leaves that make it attractive. Early cutting may yield weak stems, but later in the year, when the stems become woody, sage is nearly indestructible, not to mention plentiful. This crop tends to flop, so you might want to net it. We don't, as it's so prolific we can waste a few stems, and when the center stems, which are straighter, are cut, the curved outer stems tend to move toward the center and straighten up! Either of these sages takes the place of traditional greenery and designers of all sorts use it in large amounts for table setting and other situations.

If you have a grasshopper problem on your farm, you'll see it first on sage, their favorite foliage. You'll need to spray every week, before a problem occurs. You may be able to sell flowers with damaged leaves but foliage is not so forgiving and you can lose a crop in a few days to just a few hungry grasshoppers.

We were in business for almost two decades before we discovered Dusty Miller. Long lasting in the vase, it's loved by most clients, and being relatively pest-free (we've not discovered a problem yet) it's loved by us. It's short, so we only grow it inside in hoophouses or greenhouses where it reaches eighteen inches tall, but if it's planted early from plugs it produces two cuttings, up to half a bunch per plant per cutting. At eight dollars a bunch that's sixteen hundred dollars for a thirty dollar investment for plants—a slightly better return than Enron stock. We like the round leaf form "New Look", but other varieties like "Silver Dust" seem just as popular.

Artemisia Silver King provides a constant source for silver-gray foliage. As soon as the stems seem stiff and woody start cutting, and continue cutting throughout the rest of the season. Cut back part of the crop when it's only a foot or so tall so you have a later harvest for August and September, since you don't really want it to seed out. As with most prolific rhizomes, you'll want to plant this in an area you can keep under control. We have it in a bed bordered by walkways and we spray glyphosate on the edges when the Silver King creeps out toward nearby perennials. Very heavy mulching or tilling may also keep this Artemisia at bay. Silver King generally escapes insect pressure, but Painted Lady caterpillars sometimes find it desirable early in the season and aphids occasionally stop by—they don't stay, but they do use it as a momentary resting spot early in the year so sometimes evade our scrutiny until a client alerts us (that's embarrassing).

WOODIES

A cold climate limits the number of useful woodies to be grown, and alkaline soil shrinks the list even further, but these are some we've tried and had success with—and a number we've tried that ended up in failure.

Aronia. Known as chokeberry, Aronia grows slowly and sports dark, almost black berries late in the summer that evade birds' interest but which last well and command designer appeal. A very good producer, once established.

Chokecherries. We grew these for private use for nearly a decade before the light bulb came on and we realized they'd make a great cut. We always loved the fragrant blossoms in spring but knew they didn't hold at all, so abandoned them to harvest for syrup and jelly in late summer (except the birds always beat us to the berries, and we were too tired and busy to pick them, anyway). But when we cut a few stems of the just swollen green berries and tried them in a vase, we knew we'd struck gold. We sold every usable stem but the birds must have been watching, because they suddenly started going after the green berries when for years they'd waited for them to turn purplish black and sweeter. Now we have to cover the chokecherries immediately after bloom. Coppicing may be a useful technique for this crop.

Forsythia. There's a constant market for Forsythia, but we can't keep a constant supply. It buds early during erratic winter warm spells, which come nearly every year (if they come every year, is it erratic?), so the buds freeze once the cold returns, leaving us with no harvest. You can cut Forsythia and force it in the cooler, but our cooler is full of tulips at that time so we lack room for the bulky stems. The foliage is useful later in the year and may be a better bet for those in northern climes.

Hydrangea. Only a couple Hydrangeas find use in our cold climate, since Macrophyllas bloom on second year wood whose buds always freeze here. Paniculatas grow on same year stems, so Annabelle, Limelight and PeeGee sometimes succeed in cold zones, though neither of the latter two like our farm's alkaline soil and rarely bloom. Annabelle does well and blooms prolifically, and while growers from more appropriate climates may laugh at our harvest, clients find our smaller blooms more useful than the pumpkin sized heads they normally see. Cut these well into maturity but before they turn brown, and shear to the ground in late winter to promote long and perfect stems.

Lilacs. Syringa Vulgaris (Lilac) provides one of the earliest flowers of the season. Not every lilac throws a usable cut flower stem, so research this carefully before planting useless ones (as we did when we bought some "late flowering" lilacs we thought would extend the season, but, while blooming prolifically with very large inflorescences, last only a day or two in a vase). From even a two by two pot, a lilac will be harvestable at three years of age, so brings a quicker return than most woodies. After flowering, deadhead the uncut blooms, cutting deeply to inspire longer stems the following year. Expect late, ill-timed frosts to abort flowers on years when spring comes early.

Osier. A large grower in the East convinced me to grow Osiers, citing their ease of growing and long harvest window, and I planted three varieties, a burgundy stem, a fuchsia, and a yellow (that turns a very nice green just before leafing out in the spring). We found we didn't have enough customers to justify our plantings, though, and pulled our crop from the ground after a decade. Osiers need to be cut back in order to grow straight stems, so if you don't harvest all of them you still put in many hours of pruning (unless you have a mechanical device that cuts woodies). If you have lots of customers, however, or a good wholesaler you can sell lots of stems to, this is an easy crop. We find the yellow variety to be much more desirable than the others, but that might just be our clientele.

Philadelphus. Known as Mockorange, this species caught our eye only recently. Fragrant with an early season bloom, it comes during June wedding time and finds almost universal use.

Physocarpos. Physocarpos Diablo and its brethren find favor from most of our clients. Our favorite Physocarpos occurs when specific plants, after several years, revert to a green leaf, rather than the dark, burgundy-black they normally sport, but the green-leafed ninebark we've found at nurseries doesn't have the long stem and large leaf as the chimeras we're looking for. We'll just have to wait for more plants to revert to their roots.

The best ninebark stems come when you trim the shrub severely in the spring, almost to the ground, but usable, later stems grow even from prior year's growth. Last year's uncut stems flower in early June (new Physocarpos stems do not flower) quite spectacularly but shatter, and so find use only for events, and the seed heads can be a brilliant red if pollinated evenly, giving yet another use. Between the flowers, seed heads and foliage Physocarpos has a long season of giving that begins in late spring and continues past first frost. We haven't seen an insect pest on Physocarpos in twenty years of growing it, but from time to time powdery mildew shows up so monitor plants in areas protected from the winds.

Quince. We love the look of Quince, but find it nearly impossible to cut. No matter what you do in terms of pruning, you can't really force it to make a straight stem as you can with Forsythia, Lilac or Viburnum, so your bunches are scraggly, multi-branched and bulky, taking a lot of room in the cooler and on the truck. That bulkiness, however, fills up an arrangement well, making Quince a real prize for designers. The flowers last very well in a vase.

Roses. We grow only David Austin roses—their shape and fragrance trumps their short vase life when used for events. You can use these many-petaled "cabbage" roses to fake a peony when peonies aren't available. Though they seem expensive to plant, if you really want to get your money back quickly you can cut them the first year and recover your costs, but if you'll be patient and think long term, just deadhead them the first year and reap twice as many in subsequent years. We get a second bloom in mid to late August here, though if any particular plant looks like it's weakening we refrain from harvest, and rarely do we throw many away the demand is so great.

If you're a fussbudget or don't mind the extra work, cover your roses with a loose mulch that protects them from biting winds and frost yet allows air through to alleviate fungal pressure. We work under the "tough love" system, however, and make them suffer the consequence of weather despite the threat of their demise. The loss rate hovers at less than ten percent even on years of nasty winters, and our initial planting of Austins from ten years ago remains a good harvest.

Charles Darwin is Jeriann's favorite Austin, by far, sporting a popular antique ivory color here in high light conditions and surviving continuous cutting over the years, while Pat Austin is a dud because of its poor vase life—barely two days, when the typical four days of other Austins is already pretty short.

We were excited about Kordes roses, bred as they are for fragrance, when they initially came out in the United States, but found that most didn't excite our clients. Though many of the tea rose varieties bloomed prolifically, almost beyond belief, they look too much like other roses easily imported on the cheap. And the Kordes varieties most similar to Austins performed poorly, as did those bred for their hips, which fruited too late for our marketing season.

Wait to prune rose canes until the last frost danger passes, then snip to the green stem. To make cleanup easier, lay netting nearby to put cut canes on, then roll up the netting for discarding. Otherwise, the thorny stems will be a nuisance, capable not just of drawing blood at a touch but of flattening a tractor tire.

Viburnum. There should be a Keatsian ode to Viburnum, particularly the lacecap version Trilobum, as virtually no plant we grow has such great design appeal, vase longevity, long cutting season, commands a high price and is easy to grow, to boot. Its only problem comes from a susceptibility to aphids very early in the season when frosty nights still occur, before I'm actually paying attention to pest control outside the greenhouses.

Snowball Viburnum especially succumbs to aphids, sometimes an entire crop being lost from discolored flowers and curled leaves. Supposedly spraying dormant oil curtails the aphid problem, but my use of the oil resulted in no check at all the times I used it. Systemic insecticide no doubt would work, but I just take my chances and lose a crop from time to time thinking that in the long run it all evens out since the shrubs, given a break from cutting, will be that much more vigorous, and I, given an equal break, will be that much more grateful when the stems increase in number.

Viburnums, like most early flowering shrubs, bloom on second year stems, so heavy pruning immediately after flowering increases next year's harvest a great deal—cut back multi-stemmed branches that obviously won't yield sufficiently long stems, and cut them deep. Viburnum holds well in the cooler. We're not afraid to hold it for three weeks for those late June weddings.

You'll likely not sell all the Viburnum you grow as flowers, but no worry. In just about a month the berries that form from pollinated flowers firm up enough to sell, even though they're still green, and from there on out you can sell them the rest of the summer as they turn yellow, then as they get tinged a coffee-ish brown, and then when they become red. Nothing we grow, save foliage plants, has a longer cutting season.

Excited by the Viburnum yield, we experimented with a number of other Viburnums, including Viburnum Prunifolium Blackhaw (the stems grow more like Quince rather than straight), Viburnum Dilatatum Erie (better as foliage—earlier by a few days, but duskier white bloom), Viburnum Lantana Mohican, Viburnum Emerald Triumph, and Viburnum Cassinoides Witherod (a total disaster). Due to an accident of the nursery that sent us our initial Viburnum Trilobum, we have one rogue Viburnum with big yellow berries when ripe which surpasses even our favorite varieties, but we have no idea what it is—though we know it's not Michael Dodge, which has failed to thrive (it barely survives) here in our alkaline soil.

We once grew Viburnum Blue Muffin and even voted for it as Plant of the Year. The crop we had on our first rented land sported huge clusters of grape-colored berries that walked off the truck as soon as the doors opened, but the next set of plants we put in the new land have yet to yield a single usable stem, though we occasionally cut it as a bloom since it follows Trilobum season by about a week. Plantsmen from the company where we bought our plants claimed we needed another variety as a pollinator (we didn't have one on our first planting, but THEY bloomed) and recommended Chicago Lustre, which we discovered blooms two weeks later than Blue Muffin and couldn't possibly aid in berry set, being a bit late to the party. The mystery's yet to be solved, though many growers throughout the nation make the same complaints about non-fruiting.

Viburnum blooms on last year's wood, so prune early in the year to give next year's stems plenty of time to lengthen.

THE TOOLS

Netting may rival rebar as a flower farm's primary technology, and since they almost always find their use in unison we can call their rivalry a tie. In the coddlesome environs of a greenhouse where plants get no exercise but grow taller and weaker than their street-tough, outside brethren, a single floppy stem can topple and set an entire bed down with a domino effect. So, netting becomes a requirement for almost all greenhouse crops, even short ones like Dusty Miller and sage that barely hit fifteen inches. While the support system for the netting (made by Hortonova) can be as elaborate as you wish, rebar and T-posts keep ours upright.

Most varieties need a post every four or five feet and another on the opposite side to stretch the netting tight, but very tall crops like Snapdragons may need a set every two feet to keep side to side motion at a minimum, and another set of supports in the middle to stop sway that moves end to end. Greenhouse snaps need two layers of netting, in fact, a requirement few other species claim.

Outside, where wind makes stems stronger and less shade keeps plants shorter, less support is necessary. For very large plants like dahlias, however, T-posts and netting are essential.

In almost all cases, netting increases cutting difficulties exponentially. Reaching through with one hand (do I reach over or do I reach under?) and pulling stems through with another (do I pull up, or do I pull down?), it seems as if another set of arms might be necessary. Crops like Bells of Ireland (grown indoors, we don't net outdoor Bells) and Dusty Miller may be so entangled that cutting the netting and removing the shredded pieces makes the job easier.

Felco pruners do the best job cutting shrubs and field bunches (and poly tubing, but don't tell Jeriann), while smaller flowers cut best with bonsai scissors. We use florist knives to cut sunflowers and Amaranth, sliding the blade down each side of the stalk (pointed slightly away from the stalk to avoid slicing into it) to remove leaves, then slashing an angled cut at the desired stem length.

We bunch using #19 rubber bands for small flowers and #32 for large ones, and use grocery ties to wrap around the necks of sunflower bunches, osier, allium and grasses to keep them disentangled.

Plastic flower sleeves are a necessary evil, with different sizes used for different flowers and never enough sizes to fit the number of species. As the cut flower industry has diminished, so has the number of sleeve suppliers and number of sizes of sleeves, so generally you just have to go with the best rather than with what would work perfectly. We find microperforated sleeves breathe best, keeping dampness and mold from forming, but sometimes settle for perforated sleeves that often come in slick plastic more difficult to use. Satin sleeves work well for the processor, but make visualizing the flowers in them difficult. Without sleeves to differentiate bunches, customers can't tell what they're purchasing. Too nice or too timid to ask, they may pass unbunched flowers by—we discovered this when we took a bucket of quaking grass on the truck and sold none, then sleeved them and sold them all the next trip.

Useful herbicides include 2-4-D amine (never buy ester, which drifts badly) and everyone's evil, glyphosate. When we spray borderlines and roads we often use them together as the former works on broadleafs and the latter works on grasses. Poast works on grass problems, and carefully used can be sprayed over most broadleafs without damaging them—but if you put too much oil with it, the oil can kill the plants. If you wait until a weed has reached bud stage to spray, don't spray at all, you'll be wasting your time and chemical, as most plants, once in bud, continue to make seed.

Pesticides we use include Tempo, which works on root weevil, Bifenthrin, which seems to be the only over the counter chemical that kills spider mites, and Malathion for aphids. We prefer not to use chemicals and refrain from doing so whenever possible, but in a highly agriculturalized area like ours bug problems can become so widespread that applicators sometimes must wipe insects from their windows at each turn just to see. My first method of dealing with insects is always panic, after which I try the above.

A number of fungicides that work to varying degrees are available over the counter and should be alternated in use. Most fungicides only work if you catch the problem early, so scout your farm regularly, eyeing suspect species first. Potato growers use Equus for blight here and many tulip growers use it for Tulip Fire.

On a bucket route, Square is an essential financial tool. Given that the world's gone completely electronic, having Square available to complete credit transactions on your smart phone makes business much easier than waiting for a client to find checkbooks and write out checks while her customers wait on her. Cheaper than Visa and Mastercard (and, needless to say, American Express), Square will bring in more money than it costs just because it simplifies things. Twenty percent of our payments go through Square. Why make buying your product difficult?

You can purchase as many tractor implements as you desire. We get by, however, with a chisel plow (three rows of shanks, each with a duck foot, all offset) for working ground without plant matter on it (which clogs the plow), a rotovator, a one shank ripper that cuts through the plow pan that eventually forms from regular tillage, and a drip tape layer. We have a pull behind roller, a tape lifter, and we did have a fertilizer spreader until we forgot to clean it—fertilizer rusts metal so now we have an artifact with frozen gears. Buy a fiberglass seeder/spreader to avoid this problem. A rotary mower helps with cutting large swaths of plant material back (do clean up in the late fall if you have vole problems, but otherwise in the spring to give plants a better winter survival rate), while a weed whacker of some sort suffices for smaller areas.

You can get by without a loader, until you have one. We leave ours off all summer, however, and just use it for moving mulch and sludge in the fall and spring. We have a sprayer, but don't use it some years. Backpack sprayers, one for herbicides, one for fungicides and pesticides (label the two and don't ever use one for the other), are essential, though difficult to use in small spaces like the greenhouse. We bought a motorized backpack sprayer but seldom use it, as it weighs nearly seventy pounds when filled, a bit much even for the triathlete we employ.

If you have greenhouses, you need a rototiller. Four or five horses is big enough, and six may be too much. Ours, a Husqvarna, does a good job but is a beast to operate compared to the old Troy-Bilt we had. A small roller to compress the soil comes in handy, too.

Fertilizer injectors work for dripline infusions. For smaller areas like greenhouses, the EZ Flow works well as a hookup to a regular garden hose (be sure you have backflow devices installed to prevent chemical from entering your well or water source). Larger units get quite spendy, and while we purchased an expensive Mix-Rite, which operates with water pressure, we find that it so hinders water flow that we prefer not to use it. Electric pump types no doubt perform their job without interfering with pressure.

As far as tools go, we have a couple adjustable end wrenches, some screwdrivers, some waterpump pliers and regular pliers, some sockets, a hammer, a post pounder for T-posts, assorted hoes and shovels, a soil knife for taproot weeds, an air compressor for tires and a battery charger. There may be a few other assorted tools but since I wouldn't know how to use them if I had them, I stay away from purchasing more.

So, I hope the whole venture of flower farming doesn't sound like it's too hard to try, but if it does maybe it's a good thing you read this book, anyway. I don't think there are many out there who will start with less of everything needed than we possessed when we started(except ignorance and uncertainty), so you may begin believing you can do it. Do your homework, experiment, have knowledge of yourself and faith IN yourself, and you'll succeed. We did.

Eventually, that is.

Now go eat that elephant.

Printed in the United States
By Bookmasters